CLASSICS OF RUSSIAN POETRY

Lermontov

The Demon and Other Poems

"Translators are the post-horses of civilization."
—*A. S. Pushkin (1830)*

by the same author

Pasternak	POEMS, 2nd edition, revised and enlarged
Pushkin	EUGENE ONEGIN
Pushkin	LITTLE TRAGEDIES
Pushkin	TSAR SALTAN & OTHER FOLK TALES

Mikhail Yuryevich Lermontov (1814-1841)
portrait by K. A. Gorbunov, 1839

MIKHAIL LERMONTOV

The Demon and Other Poems

translated from the Russian
by Eugene M. Kayden

Introduction by
Sir Maurice Bowra

The Antioch Press, Yellow Springs, Ohio • 1965

Acknowledgment. As translator of Lermontov's poetry, I am grateful to the Carnegie Foundation for the financial assistance which it has given to the general program of research and creative work at the University of the South. I am delighted for the opportunity to acknowledge the timely help in my own case.

E. M. Kayden

All rights reserved. No part of this book may be reprinted in any manner without written permission, except in the case of brief quotations in critical articles.

Copyright 1965 by Eugene M. Kayden. Library of Congress Catalog Card No. 62-21070. Printed in the United States of America by The Antioch Press, Yellow Springs, Ohio.

To

FLORENCE E. TEAGER

dedicated

to friendship

Contents

Mikhaíl Lérmontov . . . . *frontispiece*
Lérmontov in Fatigue Cap x
Introduction xi

EARLY ROMANTIC POEMS

Monologue 3
Do You Remember How Together. 4
Melody 5
This World of Loveliness 6
A Foreboding 7
The Warrior's Grave 8
My Home 10
Tides 11
Hope 12
The Cup of Life 13
The Angel 14
I'm Not a Byron 15
Nevermore We Shall Meet 16
A Sail 17
The Reed 18
Circassian Song 20
The Mermaid 21

FROM ROMANTICISM TO REALISM

The Dying Gladiator 25
Borodinó 27
The Poet's Death 31
The Palm of Palestine 34
The Prisoner 36

My Neighbor	37
When Fields of Rye Wave Golden	38
Supplication	39
We Parted	40
I Should Not Like the World to Know	41
When Your Voice I Hear	42
The Dagger	43
Before I Leave For Home	44
Meditation	46
The Poet	48
O Dreamer, Disbelieve Your Dream	50
Three Palms	52
Prayer	55
The Gifts of Terek	56
In Memory of Alexander Odóyevsky	59
New Year's Night	62
I Am Lonely and Sad	64
Cossack Cradlesong	65
The Captive Knight	67
Wherefore	68
Gratitude	69
Mountain Heights	70
Lines to a Child	71
To A. O. Smirnóva	73
To a Portrait	74
Clouds	75
Farewell to Russia	76
Valerík	77
The Testament	84
Vindication	86
My Native Land	87
A Dead Man's Love	88

Agreement 90
The Cliff 91
The Dispute 92
A Dream 96
Tamára 97
The Rendezvous 99
An Oak Leaf 102
Lone I Walk at Night 103
The Princess of the Sea 104
Not For You My Love 106
The Prophet 107

NARRATIVE POEMS

The Lay of Kaláshnikov the Merchant 111
The Fugitive 129
The Novice 134
The Demon 159

Translator's Note—The verse translations, including dates, are based on the edition of Lermontov's complete poetry in four volumes, edited by B. M. Eikhenbaum, published by ACADEMIA in 1936. A few revised dates are taken from D. Maksimov's edition in two volumes, published by SOVETSKI PISATEL in 1957. The contents of each section are arranged chronologically.

LERMONTOV IN FATIGUE CAP
Pencil drawing by D. I. Pahlen, 1840, made after the engagement at Valerik

Introduction

Within a few days of Pushkin's death on 29 January 1837 the reading public of St. Petersburg was presented with a poem called *The Poet's Death,* written by a Hussar officer in the Imperial Guard who was twenty-two years old and called Mikhail Lermontov. If this poem begins as a lament for the sudden destruction of a great genius, it ends as a fierce rebellious denunciation of the Russian ruling classes, and especially of the parasites who swarm round the throne and murder freedom, genius, and glory, and warns them that vengeance will fall upon them. Lermontov was stirred by a justifiable suspicion that Pushkin's death had been desired by the court and that Tsar Nicholas I was not displeased by it. *The Poet's Death* soon came to the notice of the authorities, especially of Count Benckendorff, who had long harried Pushkin and was quick to detect any criticism which savoured of indiscipline. Lermontov was first put under arrest and then exiled to the Caucasus. He did not stay there long, but was back in St. Petersburg before the end of 1838. But this outbreak into politics marked a crisis in his career. Henceforward the young officer, known chiefly for his difficult temper and vagrant amours, was marked equally by those who watched with eager expectancy for any new manifestation of Russian poetry and by those who kept suspicious guard against any

---

The introduction reproduces the essay on Lermontov by Sir C. Maurice Bowra, here reprinted with few excisions from *Inspiration and Poetry* (London, Macmillan & Company, 1955) by permission of publisher and author.

symptoms of intellectual independence. More than this, it was a turning-point in Lermontov's own career. With the death of Pushkin he discovered the full measure of his poetical calling From now onwards until his death in 1841 he wrote with an accomplished mastery and a secure knowledge of his capacities. The mantle of Pushkin had fallen on him, and he was confident of his ability to wear it worthily.

Though the collected works of Lermontov contain a bulk of poetry surprisingly large for a man who died at the age of twenty-six, yet he himself was slow to publish and published only what satisfied his own highly exacting standards. In his lifetime he published his novel, *A Hero of Our Time,* and one volume of lyrical verse, which contains only twenty-eight poems out of the 400 and more which he is now known to have written, and includes among these twenty-eight four translations from German or English. Lermontov was an extremely severe critic of his own work and passed nothing which he did not think to be as good as he could make it. It is unfair to judge him by the whole bulk of his work. Much of it is undeniably sentimental and imperfect, but what else is to be expected from a boy still in his teens? At the same time, even among the pieces which he himself did not think worthy of publication are some which have won an enormous popularity and are known to every Russian. He was by nature an abundant writer who controlled his abundance with searching criticism, and in any judgment on him we should remember that he was himself the harshest judge of his own work. He lived no longer than Keats, and, like Keats, he did not find his full powers before the last four or five years of his life, but, unlike Keats, he did not hurry into print but waited until he was certain that he had done his best.

Lermontov's life concerns us only so far as it explains his poetry. Like Pushkin, he came from the lesser nobility and claimed a long and distinguished ancestry. His mother died when he was a small child, and the affection which he lost in her was not adequately replaced by the attentions of his grandmother. He had an excellent education, spoke French like a Frenchman and was well at home in German and English. But when he went to the University of Moscow, he benefited little by it, did not make the acquaintance of distinguished fellow students like Belinsky and Konstantin Aksakov, and kept aloof in haughty contempt for the fine talk of his contemporaries. In 1834 he became an officer of Hussars and flung himself into the smart, fast life of the capital. After his return from exile in 1838 he continued to cause anxiety to the authorities. In 1840 he was punished for a duel with Ernest de Barante, the son of the French ambassador, by being sent into exile again to the Caucasus, returned towards the end of the year, and then went back to the Caucasus, where on 15 July 1841 he was killed in a duel, in which he did not attempt to defend himself, by a friend, Major Nikolai Martynov, whom he had infuriated by his gibes. In the intervals of pleasure, lovemaking, military service, in which he acquitted himself with great distinction, Lermontov wrote his poetry. He died at the same age as Keats, but unlike him he showed no signs of slackening powers at the end. . . .

Unlike Pushkin, Lermontov did not pass weeks and months in bored idleness only to burst into inexplicable, unforeseen flights of creative activity. In his busy life he wrote poetry whenever occasion allowed, even in the intervals of battle. When the impulse came to him, he would emend his first draft with remorseless excisions and inspired corrections. . . . With all his abundance, Lermontov was so good a critic that he was able to hoard his best lines until he could put them to a truly appropriate use.

In the eyes of his keener contemporaries and of his countrymen ever afterwards Lermontov inherited the mantle of Pushkin and began where the dead poet ended. In 1840 Belinsky said of him: 'In that young man a third Russian poet is getting ready, and Pushkin did not die without an heir.' There is truth in this if we take it to mean not that Lermontov continued to work in the same way as Pushkin but that he followed his own temperament to develop much that Pushkin had begun. This is certainly the case with his style. Pushkin's style, with its simplicity and its strength, its effortless variety and tremendous charge of emotion, taught Lermontov how to write. He too makes every word do its work and every line say all that it can. But if Pushkin is simple, Lermontov is simpler still. He conforms, as very few poets do, to Wordsworth's prescription for the language of poetry, and does it with so unassuming an air that we hardly notice his style as such, so perfectly wedded is it to his mood and his purpose. Every word comes so inevitably and so naturally into the sentence that we mark not the choice of words but their final effect. But of course this is a triumph of style. Hardly any poets have written with quite this ease and self-effacing simplicity, and yet succeeded in being powerful and expressive. Lermontov lacks Pushkin's caressing sweetness and gift for suggesting a whole complex mood, but he almost makes up for it by a sheer force which strikes us directly as a powerful response to experience. When early in the present century advanced Russian poets, eager to exploit neglected qualities of their language, claimed that Pushkin was too sweet and too Italian, they did not say the same of Lermontov, whom they regarded as a more masculine, more forcible writer. The judgment is hardly just when we think of *Poltava* or *The Bronze Horseman*, but there is an element of truth in it in so far as it stresses Lermontov's concentrated force and confidence.

This style Lermontov applied to an extremely personal experience. Like Pushkin, he wrote about himself and his emotions and knew nothing stronger than his aching desire for liberty. But he was born fifteen years after Pushkin and looked on the world with fewer and fainter hopes. He never knew the fervour for reform which ended so catastrophically with the failure of the Decembrist revolt in 1825, and for him the call of the French Revolution was lost in an irrecoverable past. He grew to manhood in the police-state of Nicholas I, when any independence was likely to be punished and finer spirits suffered from a conviction of futility and impotence. By nature he was a rebel, if not in a political sense, at least against the crassness and cruelties of the established order, and it is significant that, when he was a child, he would brandish his fists at his grandmother for maltreating her serfs. Like Pushkin, he longed for some unattainable freedom in which he could be uncompromisingly himself without checks or obligations, but he was born too late to think that this was even conceivable. Whatever he might desire in the depth of his being, he was convinced that he would never find it and that he was trapped in a way of life from which there was no release. This conviction, which was fully justified, was strengthened by something which had troubled him since childhood, a vague sense of homesickness for some lost happiness, a 'hunger for eternity', a longing for a supernatural exaltation. In *The Angel*, written when he was sixteen, he gives expression to this feeling and sets forth the fancy that the soul at birth hears an angel's song and is ever afterwards haunted by it.

This sense of frustration fostered a deep discontent in Lermontov and led him even in youth to two almost inconsistent positions, a fierce scepticism and a no less fierce desire for action. The first is common enough in imaginative youth, but Lermontov held it with an uncommon force. In *The Cup of Life* he expresses with memorable pathos a sensitive schoolboy's sense of unreality in everything around him, and tells how, as we drink from the cup of life, the brim is wet with our tears until death comes and shows that it is all an illusion. . . . To escape from his melancholy uncertainties Lermontov sought excitement and adventure both in life and in imagination. The main lines on which he was to move were set in boyhood, and to them he remained constant.

Externally Lermontov was a man of the world, a frequenter of high society, feared and disliked for his cruel jokes, the author of ribald verses, the reckless, inconstant lover, the poet who claimed to have no interest in his poetry and refused to talk about it. This appearance was much more than a pose. . . . At least this was how his contemporaries saw him. These elements were certainly in his nature and at times entered into his poetry. But behind this outer self was another, more human and more interesting. So Belinsky, who was among the first to divine Lermontov's genius, and visited him when he was under arrest in 1837, found a man quite different from what he expected:

> The first few minutes I felt awkward, but later we somehow got engaged in a discussion of English literature. . . . I looked at him and could not believe my eyes or my ears. His face assumed such a natural expression; he was his own self for the moment. There was so much truth and simplicity in his words! For the first time I saw the gentle Lermontov, such as I have always wished to see him.

When he was away from society, for which he had adopted a protective colouring, Lermontov was a different man, and a simpler, more natural self emerged behind the hard-bitten man of the world.

In his contradictions Lermontov shows a remarkable resemblance to Byron. In both we find a touch of the cad and the rake countered by genuine tenderness and affection; an affectation of contempt for their own poetry because they were afraid that others might despise it; a way of deriding much that in their best moments they treated seriously; a respect and a liking for high society which was poorly dissimulated under a contempt for it but matched by sudden longings for solitude and the companionship of nature; an insistence on their noble birth and a liking for simple peasants or warlike barbarians in Greece or Georgia; a zest for pleasure in many forms and an ability to endure hard conditions by considerable self-denial; an abundant vitality combined with an appetite for danger and a disregard for death. No doubt this similarity was partly due to similarities in upbringing and social circumstances. Both seem to have been starved of maternal affection in childhood and to have been dubious whether any real love could last or even exist; both were welcomed by high society, only to find themselves despised or ostracised by it; both longed to be fully and freely themselves in a world dominated by strict rules and conventions. But these similarities are matched by differences no less important. Unlike Byron, Lermontov never woke up to find himself famous, never enjoyed a handsome income from his books, never got away from a mode of life which he detested to choose another which suited him, never established relations with a woman comparable to Byron's with La Guiccioli. Greater than these differences in their lives are the differences in their work. Though Lermontov had indeed the Byronic temperament, though he read and admired Byron and learned something from him, his poetry is quite independent. He never admits to it the kind of wit which he practised so recklessly in his life and which Byron used so gloriously in *Don Juan*. When he wrote poetry, Lermontov shed his social self and became a different man. Moreover, Byron took very little trouble with his poetry, poured it out in careless abundance, and left it at that, but Lermontov was an extremely conscientious and critical artist, who worked hard on every word and was content only with his very best. The result is that we think of him more as a poet than as a personality, or at least as a personality only because he is a poet.

Lermontov's poetry reflects his conflict with himself. He was cynical because he felt that the world had defeated him. In boyhood he had longed for some ideal, unattainable condition, and, when he failed to find it, he compromised with the world and treated it, as he thought it deserved, by going further than most men in the reckless, hard-hearted spirit which prevailed in society. But behind this we can see that his cynicism was largely due to his bitter conviction that his most cherished hopes would never be fulfilled. He longed for affection, but found that women were faithless and that friends betrayed him; he was as patriotic as any Russian, but his country was governed by the sycophants of a pedantic tyrant, and he turned on them with savage indignation; he felt the lure of aristocratic life at St. Petersburg, only to find that he must listen to the hackneyed words of people without souls and be surrounded by 'masks frigid with propriety'. He had neither the experience nor the means to break with this life, and indeed there was nothing for him to do. The rigid system of the Tsars made no allowance for talent, and Lermontov was at least fortunate in being exiled to the Caucasus. Even at the front his heroic actions brought him no benefit. The Tsar ignored his citations for bravery and commendations for awards. Lermontov was inexorably condemned to a conflict between his innermost desires and the hard system which held him in captivity.

What his temperament and circumstances cost Lermontov, and what they did for his poetry, may be seen from his treatment of love. Like Pushkin, he fell in love often and wrote about it from many angles, but, unlike Pushkin, he says very little of its happiest or most tender moments. Sometimes indeed he seems to write in the moment of falling in love, but it is rather a moment of magic when he hears a beautiful voice which seems to promise everything. There is nothing in his work comparable to Pushkin's stanzas *To A. P. Kern* or *The Beauty*. Lermontov's treatment of love is more complex and more oblique. We may suspect that, when he fell in love, he never did so quite completely, because he was always troubled by fears or doubts or disturbing memories. . . . He seems to have known the full power of love only when he had lost it. Then indeed he might feel gratitude and affection, but it is for something that might have been, or for a memory which is sweet in retrospect and more real from a distance. We cannot doubt the genuine affection of such a poem as *We Parted*, but it is an affection salvaged from the past. From love Lermontov extracts a peculiar pathos, but it is the pathos of defeat and regret.

This sense of failure sometimes takes forms which are none

the less true for their strangeness and touch of violence. Even when all is well, Lermontov is troubled by fear and suspects evil ahead, as in *Wherefore*, where his sympathy and understanding for his beloved prompt a thought of what sufferings await her. No one can claim that this was written by a cynical amorist, but it was equally not written by a man who knows the sublime confidence of being in love. Even at such moments Lermontov's insecurity spoils the happy moment (*Not For You My Love*). He seems to have been possessed by an ideal of a lost love which prevented him from ever falling fully in love again. . . . No less striking is the poem *A Dead Man's Love*, in which Lermontov dramatises himself as a corpse who still thinks of his beloved and appeals to her from the grave, saying that, just as he still remembers and loves her, so should she remember and love him. It is, as it were, a counterpart to those lines which Pushkin wrote to Amalia Riznich four years after her death, reminding her of the kiss which she has promised him when they meet again. If Pushkin carries to an unusual limit the notion of a love stronger than death, Lermontov carries it still further, and differs from Pushkin by transposing his passion to an imaginary situation and making it more exotic and more sensational.

If Lermontov's tormenting uncertainties made him take a low view of life about him, they also made him take a low view of himself. So far from thinking that he was the innocent victim of a wicked world, he had few illusions about himself. He dramatised himself as a lost soul, derided by society because of some fault which he had committed. The image or myth which he found for this conviction was a demon, which personified his position. In different short poems and in the various drafts of his long poem, *The Demon*, Lermontov shows how this myth changed under his hands and passed from youthful fancies to a true record of something deep in his nature. In *My Demon*, written in 1829, the Demon is a kind of Byronic hero, whose element is storm and whose character, compounded of melancholy, bad temper, and unbelief, makes him scorn love, reject prayers, and look with indifference on blood. Two years later some of the more violent traits have disappeared, and the Demon is the poet's other self, almost his familiar spirit, who taunts him with images of perfection and presentiments of bliss to be withdrawn as soon as they are presented. Lermontov at this period hovered between two ideas, the one that he was a demon, elect of evil and proud in temper, an exile from both heaven and earth, and the other that this demon was his other self, who tormented and corrupted him but was in the last resort not his essential nature.

In the last draft of the poem, *The Demon*, finished just before his death, Lermontov tells a story which is almost autobiographical in that the Demon is his own soul with its contradictions and paradoxes. The chief character is a fallen angel who loves a mortal woman and tells her who he is: 'For I am he whom no one loves, whom every human being curses.' In a declaration of love, in which every word is a flame, he says that he has forsworn his pride and desires to be reconciled with God, to pray, to believe in the good. The woman, Tamára, yields to him and forfeits her life, but her soul is borne by angels to Heaven, because she has redeemed her sin by death, while the Demon is left, as before, in despair. This conclusion does credit to Lermontov's candour. If love were all that is needed for salvation, the Demon, no less than Tamára, should be saved. But he is not, and Lermontov shows his distrust of such romantic notions. His Demon remains as he is, because, in his pride and his passion, he is incapable of sacrifice, and redemption comes not to every kind of love but only to that kind which fulfils itself in sacrifice. The Demon is Lermontov's image of his dissatisfaction and disgust with himself, of his conviction that some final weakness of flesh or character prevents him from making the sacrifice which would deliver him from his worst impulses. His Demon is a new conception of evil. He is no Satan or Mephistopheles, as Milton or Goethe created them. He is closer to the ordinary human heart with its selfish passions, its uncontrolled appetites, its cowardly refusals, its cold absorption in itself.

In his melancholy and his misgivings Lermontov had one thing to which he could hold—his art. In the last four years of his life he strengthened and enriched it in every poem. He found the Caucasus more inspiring than St. Petersburg with its uneasy pressure of social relations. Like Pushkin, he felt free among the mountains and their primitive inhabitants, savoured with relish the local stories, and enjoyed a solitary communion with the incomparable landscape. He experimented with new metrical effects, as in *The Novice*, in which he abandons the Russian fondness for feminine endings and uses masculine endings throughout, thus giving to his verse a hardness of outline not to be found in Pushkin. His imagery, always bold for his time, becomes bolder, as when he compares the Caucasus to a giant leaning on his shield or the river Terek to a lion shaking its mane. In composition Lermontov found the security which was his most urgent need. In it he was in command of himself and at peace with his circumstances. The more final and flawless a poem was, the greater was his triumph over his personal obstacles.

Lermontov's progress in mastering himself went further than this. Though he continued to write about his own problems and conflicts, he moved surely and confidently towards a more objective art. His early poetry is almost entirely about himself, even when it takes the form of drama or narrative, but in his later work he begins to create worlds which live in their own right and need no reference to his feelings or circumstances. In this progress he was helped by his growing command of his art and his increased trust in himself. A good example of it can be seen in his treatment of nature. In his early poetry nature plays very little part, and, when it does, it is as a background or a parallel to his feelings. But in the Caucasus he found a new approach to it and welcomed a companionship which made him forget his troubles in an unalloyed delight. Nature gave him the contrast which he needed to himself, and this explains his unusual treatment of it. He was not concerned with the 'pathetic fallacy' which attributes human feelings to natural things; he did not, like Wordsworth, find among mountains and lakes a philosophy of life; he had nothing in common with his contemporary, Tyutchev, who saw nature rent between light and darkness, between order and chaos; he lacked Hölderlin's vision of a radiant world still hallowed by Hellenic gods. For him the claim of nature was precisely that it is not human, that it has nothing in common with man. That was why he was at home with it (*When Fields of Rye Wave Golden*). Lermontov never goes further than this, but even this shows how careful and rational his treatment of nature is. He is content that it should be itself and so delight his eyes and ears that he asks for nothing else.

From this loving observation Lermontov learned to set the strange events of his narrative in landscapes at once majestic and real. If he shared the taste of his age for stupendous scenery, his vision of it was not half dream like Shelley's or an accumulation of fine details like Keats'. His vivid eye saw the whole scene in perspective and marked equally the main design and the significant features. If he allowed a generous measure of such description, he also made it perform an important part in his stories. One of his sublimest passages is in *The Demon*, when the Demon flies down to earth and sees the Caucasus below him, from the snow-clad peak of Kasbek, glittering like a diamond, to the rivers hurtling down rocky gorges. Here Lermontov turns a contrast which he knows in himself to stress the point of his story. The vast detachment of nature emphasises the passions in the Demon and prepares the way to his career among men. So, too, in *The Novice*, Lermontov marks the difference between the cloistered life, which his hero has hitherto led, and his sudden liberty by a contrast between the dark woods from which he emerges and the blazing scene which greets him in the heat of day. Lermontov makes nature provide an uninterested, splendidly independent antithesis to the strange ways of men and demons. It lives in its own right and gives a new dimension to the actions of which it is the stage.

Just as Lermontov transposed his own delight in nature to objective descriptions of it, so he transposed his taste for action into exciting stories. A life of gallant adventure had been his day-dream since boyhood, and it is not surprising that, when he was under arrest in 1837, he rewrote about himself some earlier lines about an anonymous hero. Even before he found his full powers, Lermontov had attempted with success themes of militant tribesmen and desperate outlaws. But his first triumph in narrative poetry was concerned with his own countrymen. In *Borodinó* (1837) he tells the story of the great battle through a soldier who took part in it, and displays a professional pride in a great achievement as well as an experienced knowledge of war. The poem is at once realistic and imaginative, detailed and exciting. It gives the authentic thrill of battle without any false glorification of it. It begins quietly with the preliminaries to the encounter, the occupation of a position suitable for defence, and the long wait before the French attack, when the soldiers sit and mend their coats or spit and clean their bayonets. Then comes the fight. This is objective narrative in the strictest sense. The old soldier speaks not in Lermontov's voice but his own, and there is nothing of Lermontov's characteristic sentiment in what he says. All that matters is a vivid experience as it might appeal to one who took part in it. The dramatisation is complete and masterly.

This art Lermontov exploited both in long and short poems. In the manner of Russian epic tales he wrote the *Lay of Kaláshnikov the Merchant* in which the old devices of narrative and the traditional metre are given a new brilliance, and an exciting and tragic tale is told without any reference to the poet's own feelings. Many shorter poems show the same art. In the *Cossack Cradlesong*, which dwells with a charming grace on the mother who rocks her child in his cradle and looks forward to the time when he will be a great warrior, her characterisation, even in so short a space, is complete and satisfying. In *The Rendezvous* the speaker is a Caucasian whose beloved has betrayed him, and the theme is the moment at night when he is about to take his revenge. In *Tamára* a witch, living in a castle which is a lifeless ruin by day and a haunt of music by night when it lures travellers to their doom, may have something in common with themes of German romanticism but owes more to Caucasian legends and has their authentic air of a world haunted by mysterious, malignant spirits. In his last years Lermontov perfected his gift for poetical narrative, showing how much can be done with a few words, some significant details, and an unfailing sense of climax. Of the poets of the Romantic period he is almost alone in the remarkable objectivity of his story-telling. Whereas Byron makes his heroes reflections of himself, or Shelley presents metaphysical abstractions in human guise, or Schiller imposes his own speculative ideas on the narrative, Lermontov tells a story for its own sake and makes the most of its possibilities by exploiting its human appeal.

Yet though he found consolation and success in the practice of such an art, Lermontov was still unhappy and troubled. His trouble was not the old Romantic melancholy or the ennui of Baudelaire. It was a pre-eminently personal problem—how could he be himself in the way that he wished when men and circumstances forbade it? The escape into art was indeed something, but it was not everything. He could not accommodate himself to his fellows, was incapable of holding his tongue, and his sharp jokes won him many enemies. He was tired of struggling with others and with himself, and inevitably his thoughts turned to some ideal state in which he would be freed from his troubles and yet still in some sense be himself. So in a poem written in the last year of his life he gives a characteristically vivid and concrete form to his desire.

As he walks on the road at night, he contrasts the serenity of the skies with his own tormented state, his longing for peace and rest. He longs to sleep and to forget (*Lone I Walk at Night*). The fancy, which Lermontov so boldly presents, reflects a mood which is not unfamiliar to young genius when it is rent by inner conflicts or finds its load of responsibility too heavy. . . . Such is the dream which young poets invent for themselves when they find the strain of life too great. It shows how they wish to secure the impossible, to maintain their imaginative vision without its cost or its cares.

This is no more than a dream. Such a state is not known to man, and it is useless to wish for it. Lermontov saw this clearly enough and with the logic of despair turned his thoughts to death. He did not desire it, as at times Shelley and Keats did, nor did he ask himself what it meant or try to persuade himself that in it he would at last be himself. He was too hard-headed to indulge in luxurious fancies of annihilation, but none the less the menace of an early death haunted him as the doom to which he was born. In such a spirit he imagines himself lying on the sands of Daghestan with a bullet through his breast (*A Dream*), while far away a young woman, who still cares for him, sees him in a vision. If Lermontov did not actively wish for death, he believed that it would soon come to him. It came soon enough, on 15 July 1841, from Major Martynov's bullet.

Lermontov has a full share of the discontent which we associate with the Romantic age. If in his ordinary life it made him sarcastic and cynical, it touched his poetry in a far more serious and more human way. Behind his self-dramatisation, behind his escapes into nature or his tales of stirring action, lay his central belief in certain things of great importance, in the affections, in truth, in courage, in liberty. He saw that what mattered so much to him mattered very little to his contemporaries, and he sought to solve the conflict by despising them, as they despised him. In the end he knew that he had failed, that his glorious message meant nothing to others. In this spirit he wrote *The Prophet*, in which at the close of his life he speaks clearly about himself. In choosing the theme and the title he had no doubt Pushkin's poem of the same title in his mind. But whereas Pushkin speaks of the ineffable splendours of the poetic calling, of the visions and knowledge which it confers, of the divine force behind it and of the infinite possibilities before, Lermontov speaks of its tragic cost, of the contempt and derision which it earns from other men. His prophet lives in the wilderness and is fed by the birds, but the contrast is absolute between his communion with God and his communion with men. Lermontov's *Prophet*, like Pushkin's, reflects a lofty conception of the poet's calling, a conception to which men of the Romantic age had been led not merely by their trust in inspiration but by their belief that poetry stands for all that is best in man and is a means to redeem the world. Lermontov did not question this belief, but a hard school taught him that it would be met by misunderstanding and obloquy and that any man who held it must pay for it with his blood.

Wadham College C. M. BOWRA
Oxford

EARLY ROMANTIC POEMS

Monologue

Believe, this dull existence forms men's lot
And bliss. . . . Of what avail our thirst for glory,
Great learning, art, our flaming love of freedom,
When still we miss their place and use in life?
Like flowers born beneath a northern sky,
A little time we bloom, but wither soon.
Dim like the winter sun on grey horizons
Our days of life, one gloomy round. Not long
The course of our unvaried, empty days. . . .
Too stifling feels the air at home; the heart
Grows heavy, and the spirit dark with grief.
In want of friendship dear and love, we waste
Our youth; our life is rotten at the core
And rank with poison stains of hate and fear.
Bitter the cup of dreary life we drink,
And naught remains that will rejoice the soul.

1829

Do You Remember How Together
(*after Thomas Moore*)

Do you remember how together
We said goodbye in evening weather?
The curfew gun boomed out at sea;
The sun went down in twilight, dying
In the heavy mist around us lying;
We heard, in anguish, silently,
The cannon boom across the tide.
How quickly o'er the gulf it died.

Today in evening light I wander
Beside the sea, and dream of you;
And when I hear the cannon thunder,
I feel our parting grief anew.
And as the dying echoes roll
In gloomy caverns of the sea,
I long, with anguish in my soul,
To share at last their destiny.

1830

The poem is a free translation of Moore's *The Evening Gun*, done in 1830, not 1841, as given in older editions. C. M. Bowra observed that Lermontov's poem is quite different in tone from Moore's, because he "made the whole sentiment less sweet and more poignant . . . closer to common speech . . . [with] a stronger climax in the end." (*Inspiration and Poetry*, pp. 178, 179.)

Melody

I gazed at a star in the heavens afar,
    In the luminous ocean of night;
Each silvery beam on the quivering stream
    Was scattered like mist in its flight.

In vain you believe all is yours to receive,
    This magic of light to enchain.
Your shadow may hide it awhile; step aside,—
    It shines in full glory again.

Thus happiness bright under cover of night
    Lures on like a phantom the mind;
It mocks with a smile, then eludes you a while,
    To glimmer again undivined.

    1830

This World of Loveliness
(from "A Fragment")

This world of loveliness and grace
Was not for us arrayed to bloom.
Our age will die without a trace
For such our fate and living doom;
In storms, upon a shoreless way,
In gloom our souls will disappear:
Our fate—to serve until the day
Of beings of a purer sphere.

They will not blight this gem of earth
Nor on social rank and gold bestow
Their spirit. From their hour of birth
In innocence their days will flow,
Free-hearted in the ways of good
On earth, in love and friendship proud.
They will not shed a brother's blood,
Indifferent, with laughter loud.

The angels as in ages past
Will speak to them in light. But we,
Enchained within a darkness vast,
Will behold their immortality;
In hatred, to the end of time
We'll watch, in woe, their paradise,—
Aware of centuries of crime
And wars aflame beneath the skies.

1830

A Foreboding

A day will come, the darkest day in all
Our time: From royal heads the crown will fall;
The mob their rulers will not love nor trust,
And you will know your heritage of lust
And death. No law will then protect the lives
Of little children and of blameless wives;
The stench of loathsome dead on every hand
And plagues that stalk throughout the mournful land
Will drive you forth from homes of death and blood;
You will be desolate with fire and flood,
Wild with cold and hunger.... And in that hour
One will appear to you, a man of power,
And you will know his face and understand
Why smokes the dagger in his mighty hand.
Woe unto you! Your moans and cries in gloom
Will be his sport upon that day of doom,
For like the vision of his lofty head
Hooded with night, your hour of dark and dread.

1830

The poem was written in the summer of 1830, a period of public disturbances and fear of peasant uprisings. It was first published in an edition of Lermontov's poetry in Berlin, in 1862.

The Warrior's Grave

An age he lies asleep in death;
　　He lies in death asleep.
Around his grave, above his mound,
　　The grasses closely creep.

The locks of the ancient warrior
　　Have mingled long with clay;
His locks shone golden in his youth,
　　At wine with comrades gay.

White his locks as the white sea foam
　　Along the curving shore;
His lips, so wise and true, are sealed
　　With cold forevermore.

Death-pale the cheeks of the warrior
　　As once his foes were pale
When he among their ranks appeared
　　In armor and in mail.

The earth bore down upon his breast,
　　But light its burden now;
The worm alone, unfearing, creeps
　　Across his death-pale brow.

Lived he for this and drew his sword
　　That, come the hour of night,
Above his lonely mound would perch
　　The eagle and the kite?

The bards his name will sing, his fame
    Age after age to keep!
For life is strong, and songs give joy!
    He lies in death asleep.

1830

My Home

My home lies wide beneath the vaulted sky
    Wherever songs of men are sounded,
And though each creature's free to occupy
    My home, I live in rooms unbounded.

How high its roof under the starry spaces,
    How far apart the distance known
From wall to wall, no mortal eye embraces,
    Except the seeing soul alone.

A greater truth the heart of man presages
    And nourishes that sacred seed
Of time: All matter, space, the tide of ages,
    His mind as in a flash will read.

For this alone my home of wondrous song
    God, the all-powerful, created,—
To be my place of grief and doom lifelong,
    And yet to be at peace, elated.

1830

Tides

In me, sublime and swift of race
    The springs of passion rise;
Their beds are silver sand; their face,
    The likeness of the skies.
The tides, undying, in a rout
Drive and whirl the sand about
    While skies in riven shrouds
    Grow gloomier with clouds.

The fountain-tides of being come
    And with each life depart;
However weak or strong in some,
    They dwell in every heart.
The weak are happy, but I know
Their empty peace I would let go
    If I could only gain
    One hour of joy or pain.

1830

Hope

I have a bird of paradise.
At dawn upon a cypress tree
She sits alone against the skies,
But sings no more by day to me.
Her back is of celestial blue,
Her head deep purple, and upon
Her wings the dust of golden hue
Reflects the brightness of the dawn.
But when the earth is slumbering
And evening mists begin to roll,
She rises on her bough to sing
So sweetly, sweetly to my soul,
That soon the burden of my pain
I fain forget before her lay,
And in my heart each tender strain
Comes as a faithful friend to stay.
Often her song so dear to me
I have in stormy weather heard:
Always of hope her song to me,
The song of my celestial bird.

1831

The Cup of Life

We drink the cup of earthly life
    With blinded eyes,
And leave about its golden brim
    Our tears and sighs.

But when at last the veil is gone,
    And death is near,
When days of sweet enchantment all
    As vain appear,—

How empty, then, we see too late,
    The cup of hours:
The wine was but a golden dream;
    The cup, not ours.

   1831

The Angel

An angel flew through the heavens of night,
    And softly he sang in his flight;
The moon and the stars and the clouds in a throng
    Came to hear the praise of his song.

He sang of the bliss of the spirits who rest
    In gardens of paradise blest;
Of the greatness of God he sang as he flew,
    And his praise rang holy and true.

In his arms he bore a young soul below
    To suffer in sadness and woe;
And, wordless, the soul remembered for long
    The strain of the heavenly song.

Long after on earth she was fated to pine,
    Aglow with a longing divine,
For sweeter than songs of the wearisome years
    The music she heard in the spheres.

1831

I'm Not a Byron

I'm not a Byron, not the same.
World-exiled, hunted everywhere,
A poet to fame unknown, I bear
A Russian soul in me aflame.
I know how brief my work will be,
How narrow in its scope and sweep;
My hopes lie shattered, coffined deep,
Like broken ships beneath a sea.
Who, dark-heaving ocean, will know
Thy mysteries, proclaim in pride
My thoughts, my dream of life below?—
Myself, or God, but none beside.

1832

Nevermore We Shall Meet

Farewell! Nevermore we shall meet,
Nevermore embrace! You are free!
Farewell! But in vain you believe
There is happiness fated to be.
I know: Your spirit will tremble
Again with passion and woe
Whenever my name will be spoken,
A name to you dead long ago.

There are sounds too scornfully heard,
Profaned as unmeaning and droll
By the crowd, but always remembered
As the intimate speech of the soul.
Our life lies entombed, deep-buried,
Enshrined in the bliss of a sound:
Two spirits alone will tremble,
Only two, at its meaning profound.

We came for a moment together,
And what's more immortal than this?
Our senses that moment lay wasted,
Consumed in the flame of a kiss.
Farewell! Do not grieve for me vainly,
Do not grieve for love and defeat:
Too bitter it seemed at parting;
More bitter our lot should we meet!

1832

A Sail

A lonely Sail afar is gleaming
Across the blue and misty sea:
What happiness, what region dreaming
Far, far from home, what destiny?

The winds cry loud; the mast is creaking
Against the flying waves at play.
No happiness the Sail is seeking—
No bliss at home, nor far away.

The sun shines gold, the sea is turning,
The sounding tide of azure glows.
Yet for a storm his wilder yearning,
As though a storm could bring repose.

1832

The Reed

Once a merry merry fisher
    Sat by a stream; before
Him slender reeds were swaying
    Along the winding shore.
The reed he cut was slender,
    The stops he made were few;
He closed one end, and into
    The other end he blew.
Then like a spirit wakened
    The reed began a strain.
It was the voice of breezes,
    It was the voice of pain.
The slender reed sang gently:
    "O life! O misery!
O merry merry fisher,
    Why do you waken me?
I was a fair young maiden,
    My cheeks were rose and snow.
In my foster mother's house
    I blossomed long ago;
But many bitter tears
    In innocence I shed,
And oft I prayed, in sorrow,
    To be among the dead.
I had a foster brother
    In manner unafraid,
A surly lad with neighbors,
    With every man and maid.
One day beside this river
    At time of evening glow,

We saw the sun go down
    And heard the waters flow.
He called me his beloved;
    My heart to him was cold.
He promised gold and riches,
    But I refused his gold.
He drew his shining dagger,
    He let me die alone;
And here my body buried
    Lies in a grave unknown.
Above my grave in secret
    Reeds quivering arose
As bodies for my sorrows,
    As veins of all my woes.
O merry merry fisher,
    O bear me gentle ruth:
No song can change my sorrow,
    Or rue my golden youth!"

1832

Circassian Song
(from "Izmail Bey")

Hail to lasses fair and bright!
In their eyes the stars of night!
If you wed, your choice is wise;
Freedom is the better prize!
    Have a care, O gallant lad,
        Never maid to wed!
    For your cash, O gallant lad,
        Buy a horse instead!

When a lad a maid will wed,
All too sad his lot ahead!
He will never join the fight,
For his wife will weep in fright!
    Have a care, O gallant lad,
        Never maid to wed!
    For your cash, O gallant lad,
        Buy a horse instead!

But your horse how true a friend
To his master to the end!
He will bear you home again
As a wind across the plain.
    Have a care, O gallant lad,
        Never maid to wed!
    For your cash, O gallant lad,
        Buy a horse instead!

1832

The Mermaid

A mermaid swam in the tremulous gleam
    Of the rising moon on a stream;
The brim of the moon she was striving to lave
    In the silvery foam of the wave.

The river, with many a shuddering cloud,
    With swirling of waters, was loud.
The mermaid sang, and the strain of her song
    On the river echoed for long.

The mermaid sang: "In our stream far away
    The sunrays quiver at play,
Where crystalline towers arise in the night,
    And goldfish gleam in their flight.

"And there on a pillow of glistening sand,
    Among reeds, in a shadowy land,
A knight in full armor lies fair in his sleep
    In the jealous heart of the deep.

"We mermaids are combing the locks of his hair,
    In the boundless dark of his lair;
We clasp as a lover the knight in the tide;
    We dance and in loveliness glide.

"Our love and caresses of passion implore
    In vain the fair knight evermore!
He sleeps in the pool of the cavernous deep,
    Nor whispers a word in his sleep."

So sang the mermaid her song on the stream
   With anguish of love in a dream;
The river, with many a shuddering cloud,
   With swirling of waters, was loud.

1832

*FROM ROMANTICISM
TO REALISM*

FROM ROMANTICISM
TO REALISM

The Dying Gladiator

> I see before me the gladiator lie.
> BYRON

Rome roars with joy. The arena hears the cries,
The thunder of applause and shouts of lust.
But he, stabbed in the heart, in silence lies
Alone, and slowly sinks in blood and dust.
In vain his troubled gaze in dying flame
Implores their mercy. Proud senator and lord
Crown one man's victory, another's shame,
And mobs, unmoved by pity and reward
Alike, the fallen hiss, and jeer his name.

His blood is running out. Each moment nearer
The fateful end, but in his vision dearer
Than life itself how wide the Danube gleams
In light, how free the summer fields! He dreams
About his children whom for war and fame
He left, his father bent by age, his wife
Who waits upon his coming home in vain,
While he, a slave, a beast for pleasure slain,
Is dying for the rabble's sport and game! . . .
Farewell, O Rome! Farewell to home and life!

O Europe, a name once glorious and dear,
The shrine of all men's dreams of joy and fear,
By struggles worn, in doubt and lassitude
You live unhonored in unfaith today,

In hopelessness, a plaything swept away,
Mocked by exulting multitudes! . . .

And now, before your last despairing hour,
With sighing deep, you muse upon your youth
In strength and light appareled, your ancient dower
Of thought neglected long, your home of truth
Blighted by luxury, by pride and power.
You thirst, in sorrow, in your hour of dying,
For old abodes, old songs, and fabled schemes,
Fantastic tales of knights and banners flying,
Flattered by vain, unwholesome, empty dreams.

1836

The two opening stanzas were taken from Byron's fourth canto of *Childe Harold*, stanzas 140-141. The poem marks the transition from literary apprenticeship to works of artistic maturity: Lermontov is now studiously realistic, renouncing negation, doubt, inaction, and devotion to some utopian past. The poem is an indictment of old Europe and its "empty dreams."

Borodinó

"But tell me, uncle, why our men
Let Moscow burn, yet fought again
    To drive the French away?
I hear it was a dreadful fight,
A bitter war, by day and night;
That's why we celebrate the might
    Of Borodinó today."—

Yes, men were heroes in the past,
Not men like you, but to the last
    The bravest in the field!
Their fate was hard, they bravely died,
And few came home by war untried.
We yielded Moscow, yet satisfied
    It was God's will to yield.

Then long we suffered in retreat,
All keen the enemy to meet.
    We muttered angry threats:
Why winter quarters? Why not reel
Them back at once? Or do we feel
We dare not let them have the steel
    Of Russian bayonets?

We found at last a stretch of land
With plenty room to make a stand!
    We built a strong redoubt.
We listened in the dark around,
Alert for every stir and sound;

Before the stars went out, we found
    The French were thick about.

I had my cannon loaded tight.
I said: I'll get you in this fight,
    My friend Mo'sieu! I say
No good for you to lurk and stall!
We'll stand against you like a wall,
And fight again, and give our all
    To bring your kind to bay!

Two days in skirmishes went by.
But all the same we grumbled why
    Lose time in trifling plays.
Our men kept saying left and right
It's time to buckle down and fight
It out!—The shadows of the night
    Came down on fields ablaze.

I dozed awhile, the guns beside,
And heard the French proclaim in pride
    Their hoped-for victory.
Our camp lay still: I heard men fret
About a battered cap, or whet
A blade, or file a bayonet,
    While grumbling angrily.

But when the morning came again,
Our camp awoke with marching men,
    Their rattling guns ahead.
Our officer was bold and brave,
A loyal fellow. Yes, he gave

His life for all of us. His grave,
    Among the nameless dead.

He called to us, with flashing eyes:
'For Moscow, for the fight! Arise!
    For Moscow we shall die
Like all the rest in battle slain!'
We'll fight and die, we cried again!
And there, upon that bloody plain,
    We kept our pledge to die.

O what a day! The Frenchmen came,
A solid mass, like clouds aflame,
    Straight for our redoubt.
Their lancers rode with pennons bright;
Dragoons came on in all their might
Against our walls, and in the fight
    They scattered in a rout.

Such wars, my lad, you'll never know!
Like shadows, banners rose, sank low,
    And rose on rampart walls.
In hiss of fire, we fought until
Our hands became too weak to kill.
The dead and wounded like a hill
    Choked the flight of balls.

That day the French found out aright
The way our Russian lads will fight
    And stand up in a war.
The earth shook loud as every breast;
Horses and men together pressed;

The fire of guns was like a vast
    And never-ending roar.

Then darkness came. Each man was true
To fight at break of day anew,
    All steadfast to the end.
'Twas then the roll of drums began.
The French fell back. We tended then
Our many wounds, and every man
    Recalled a fallen friend.

Yes, men were heroes in the past,
All daring fellows to the last
    In deeds upon the field!
Their fate was hard, they bravely died,
And few came home by war untried.
We yielded Moscow, yet satisfied
    It was God's will to yield.

1837

The Poet's Death

The poet is dead, a slave to honor,
A sacrifice to slander,—dead!
With a cry of vengeance on his lips,
He bowed at last his kingly head.
His spirit could no longer bear
Dishonor, infamy, and pain;
Alone he rose once more against
A hostile world, but now he's slain.
Slain! Of what use your grief and tears,
Your barren praise beside his tomb,
Your cringing words of vindication,
When destiny has sealed his doom?
You hounded him and long had stifled
His free and wondrous song and fame!
You fanned, for pleasure and amusement,
His silent passions to a flame!
Rejoice outright! Before the final
Sorrow his head he would not bow:
Now dark the light divine, and faded
The crown of glory on his brow.

The ruthless slayer dealt his blow
With cold and calculated aim;
His heart was blind, his hand was steady,
And straight the cruel path of flame.
Why stare in wonder, why bewildered?
An adventurer of an alien race,
He came, like other greedy seekers
After fortune and official place.
What cared he for our speech and glory,

The faith and honor of our land?
How could he know, the blind despiser,
Against whom in hate he raised his hand?

> Oh, slain! Our glory is no more!
> Like the slain hero of his story dear
> To us, the prey of jealous fear,
> The youth he sang in verses full and clear,
> Our poet is no more! . . .

Why did he leave the quiet ways of friendship plain?
Why did he seek a world where envy and disdain
The mind and heart impassioned overthrow?
Why did he clasp the hands of slanderers so base,
Believe their lying words, their false embrace,
He who from youth had learned mankind to know?

They took the poet's crown away; a wreath
Of thorn and laurel on him they laid, and now
Its hidden spines with cruel sting
Have seared his lofty brow. . . .
Designing whisperers and crafty tongues
Maddened his days, and filled with hate his rest.
And thus he died, athirst with vain revenge,
With hopes defeated in his warring breast.

> The sounds of song divine are still,
> Never on earth again to peal:
> The Singer's bed is dark and chill;
> Upon his lips, the twilight seal. . . .

* * *

But you, the spawn of worldly pride,
Breed of corruption, infamy, and shame,
And you, who crush with servile heel
The remnants of the lowly name,—
Hangmen of freedom, glory, thought,
A greedy pack who swarm around the throne,—
You hide behind the shadow of the law,
And mock at right and justice overthrown!
But God is just! A mighty judge, our God,
O men of crime! He waits!
The clink of gold will not avail!
He knows your infamies and hates!
Your slander then will help no more,
Nor will the sullen flood
Of your black gore then wash away
The poet's righteous blood!

1837

Pushkin died on 29 January, 1837, after the fatal duel with d'Anthès. Lermontov's poem of indictment was spread in thousands of hand-written copies. In the concluding 16 lines he attacked the court circles responsible for the poet's untimely death. "A call to Revolution," such was the terse comment on a copy sent anonymously to Tsar Nicholas. Lermontov was placed under arrest. In his prison, he wrote the four poems given here on pages 36, 37, 38, and 39.

The Palm of Palestine

Tell me, O palm of Palestine,
Where was your home? on what hillside?
In what green valley, of what stream,
Were you the glory and the pride?

Was it near Jordan's silver waters
Caressed by Eastern skies at dawn?
Or did wild winds of wilder night
Blow over you from Lebanon?

And as your leaves they plaited slow,
The lowly sons of Solyma,
Did they intone a quiet prayer,
In chorus sing an ancient lay?

And does the palm tree live today,
And bear aloft her leafy crown
To bless the weary traveler,
When on the waste the sun beats down?

Or did it pine like you away,
In bitter separation die?
Endure the dust of deserts round
Upon the yellow leaves to lie?

O speak! Who brought you from a land
Afar? What pilgrim saint with sighs
And prayer then held you to his breast,
And shrined you under northern skies?

Was he a consecrated knight
Who drew for God his shining sword?
And did he die, deserving grace,
Like a warrior before his Lord?

Preserved by loving care, you stand,
O palm of ancient Palestine,
Beside the icon of pure gold—
A faithful guardian of the shrine.

The evening now is soft with light;
The ark, the cross, the holy sign;
The peace of heaven dwells above,
Around you, O palm of Palestine.

1837

The Prisoner

Throw wide my prison door,
Give back the day and light,
Give back my dark-eyed maid,
And my steed with mane of night!
I will kiss, oh, tenderly
My love, my beauty shy;
Then leap upon my steed,
Through rain and tempest fly.

But, alas! the window's high,
Under lock the prison tower;
Far away my black-eyed maid
In her rich and lofty bower.
My steed, unbridled, roams
Over blossoming green leas;
He is bounding, free and gay,
And his neigh rings in the breeze.

Alone—with my grief alone.
On the bare and gloomy wall
Dim burns the icon lamp
In the hush of evenfall.
All alone; the silent sentry
Keeps watch outside my door,
And long his footsteps echo
In the gloomy corridor.

1837

My Neighbor

Dear lonely neighbor whom I cannot know,
My prison friend in suffering and woe,
   I love you as a friend of old
Remembered, though by men's design and fate
From you divided, victim of their hate,
   I never shall your face behold.

When in the twilight glow of fading day
My prison window burns with farewell ray
   Of light declining in the West,
And when the sentinel on watch beside
His post, forgetful, dreams at eventide
   Of kindliness at home and rest,

I press my forehead then against the wall,
And listen. In the gloom of evenfall
   Your song how mournful in my ears!
I cannot hear your words of breaking pain;
I can only hear the anguish of their strain
   Flow in the quiet, flow like tears.

And in my heart awakens then once more
My hope of better years that went before,
   My dream of love so long ago;
My fancies wing in regions far, unrest
In every vein, and passion in my breast,
   And tears like soundless music flow.

1837

When Fields of Rye Wave Golden

When fields of rye wave golden in the wind,
And green woods echo in the singing breeze,
And purpling berries shyly peer behind
A bush in cool-sweet shade of greening trees;

And when at dusk, or when the morning shines,
Scented with dew the lilies silver-fair
Nod languidly among the garden vines
With smiles of tender greeting in the air;

And when the brook runs bubbling in the vale
And lulls my thought in dreamland's dim repose,
While murmuring a sweet mysterious tale
To me of peaceful lands from whence it flows,

Then, calm, at peace again I slowly plod;
Then, humbled, I forget my heart's distress;
I then behold on earth my happiness,
And in the sky the face of God. . . .

1837

Supplication

Praying, I come to thee, Merciful Mother,
Heavy with sorrow, in my desolation;
Not with thanksgiving, in peril, or war,
Humbly I come to seek my salvation

Into thy presence of heavenly light.
Faint in my loneliness, wasted with passion,
All for another, a soul of true innocence,
Merciful Mother, I pray thy compassion.

Bless her with gladness who gladness deserveth,
Bless her with friends who are loyal and tender,
Grace her with youth, and thy peace that sustaineth
Grant in the winter of life to befriend her.

Then at her passing, late evening or morning,
Unto her chamber of vigil and fasting
Send to this fair one thy fairest of angels
Bearing thy love and peace everlasting.

1837

We Parted

We parted, but within my heart
I keep your image ever true;
A paling dream of days apart
And best, it brings me joy anew.

And though a slave of passion, still
My love endures: An empty shrine
Abides—a shrine upon a hill;
The idol fallen—still divine.

1837

I Should Not Like the World to Know

I should not like the world to know
My inner life and hidden grudges,
Why I have loved, and suffered woe.
Let God and conscience be my judges.

My soul will unto Him disclose
The truth and pray for consolation.
Let Him then chasten me with woes
Who first devised my desolation.

The fool's reproach, men's scorn and hate
Are vain against high souls. Forsaken
Midst howling seas and desolate,
The granite cliff remains unshaken.

His realm the raging sea and air,
His forehead stern with dark commotion;
And none his secret thought can share,
Except the thunder and the ocean.

1837

When Your Voice I Hear

When your voice I hear
So tenderly ringing,
Like a captive bird
I wake with a song.

When your glance I meet,
Your azure eyes,
My soul arises
With longing for you.

I fain would weep
In my happiness:
Oh to hold you, dear,
Close to my heart!

1837

The Dagger

I love you well, my dagger, best of friends,
My blade of steel, my comrade gleaming!
A Gruzian forged you for revengeful ends,
And tempered you, of battles dreaming.

You were a gift one tender hand once made
In trust, before my hour of leaving;
Not blood there glimmered on your shining blade
But tears—bright pearls of silent grieving.

Her dark eyes watching me in mute appeal
Were pools of grief and secret pining;
They flashed with trembling flame upon your steel,
Grew dim or bright again with shining.

Her pledge of everlasting love, this blade,
My silent comrade to the end!
I will be faithful, strong and unafraid,
Like you, like you, my iron friend!

1837

Before I Leave for Home

Before I leave for home, Kazbèk,
And hasten northward far away,
I come, O watchman of the East,
Alone within thy gorge to pray.

Since time began a shining turban
Thy wrinkled brow in snow has veiled;
Thy peace sublime and cliffs unshaken
Men in their strife have not assailed.

I come with prayer and humbly kneel
In thy retreat of snow and stone
Beneath the stars. O lift my prayer
To Allah's everlasting throne!

I pray: O send me days of coolness
On dusty trails! I ask the boon
Of quiet stone to guard my slumber
At rest in desert heat at noon.

I pray: In tempest and in thunder
Protect my weary, lonely course;
In gorge Daryál at night preserve me
And my bewildered, trembling horse.

Another prayer I have that rises
Within my yearning heart: O hear!
Am I forgotten altogether
By all my friends I hold so dear?

Will they at home embrace me gladly
With many a welcome at the door,
And will my friends as brothers greet me
Who suffered exile as before?

Or will I find among the gravestones
New graves with names of those I know—
The pure, the ardent, noble-hearted
Friends of my youth of long ago?

Kazbek, O hear and then destroy me
In thy wilds of storm and snow, alone,
And let my homeless dust lie scattered
Within thy chasm, in death unknown.

1837

Meditation

With sadness I behold our generation.
Its future's meaningless, or dark; meantime,
Crushed by new-fashioned concepts and negation,
They grow too slothful, old before their prime.
Endowed our life, before we learn to talk,
With after-wit, with follies and despair;
Our days run dull like a road we, aimless, walk,
An alien festival we cannot share.
In shame, protesting neither good nor ill,
We rot without a struggle ere we flower:
Base cowards all, in danger weak of will,
Like cringing slaves to men in power.
Thus fruit untimely ripe hangs on a tree,
Too bitter to the taste, for one brief day
Among the flowers in bloom; and, verily,
Like an orphaned thing it must at last decay.

We wasted long our minds in fruitless learning;
From closest friends and kin we hid our chief
And highest hopes, our noblest cries of yearning,
Our passion mocked by unbelief.
When scarce the cup of pleasure we attained,
Our youth was spent,—in what employ?
In fear of life and action we had drained
The vital sap from every kind of joy.

Not ours the golden dreams of verse and art
That stir sweet ecstasy. We hoard, in greed,
Mere scraps of feeling dead within the heart,
A useless treasure-trove indeed.

By chance we love, by chance we hate, but will
Not give ourselves to hate or love, entire,
Until a strange decay and chill
Consume us though our blood's on fire.
Bored by our fathers' ancient sport and story,
Their simple youthful lusts and open strife,
We go the way of death, bereft of joy or glory,
With but a snarling smile at life.

And, soon forgotten, our sullen generation
Will pass into the night, nor leave behind
One work, one thought, one word of inspiration
Devoted, out of love, unto mankind.
As citizens, our sons in future years
Will judge with rightfulness our present shame;
Our disillusioned sons with scorn and jeers
Will mock our bankrupt name.

1838

The Poet

In gold adorned my dagger on the wall gleams bright.
  A blade without a fault and trusty,
It holds the secret splendor of the East, the might
  Of tempered steel in warfare lusty.

Long years the proud companion of a man of war,
  It never asked a share of plunder;
On many a gallant breast it cut a fearful score,
  And rent the shirt of mail asunder.

More than a slave in field or banquet hall, its cold
  Steel, ringing, answered each offender;
In those brave days this dross of ornament and gold
  Had seemed a shameful, alien splendor.

On a field of combat lost, as booty borne away
  When fell its comrade unafraid,
Forgotten, in a merchant's shop the dagger lay
  Among the common wares of trade.

By war bereaved, unfriended since its comrade's fall,
  Its scabbard lost in battles gory,
Now a gilded toy it hangs neglected on the wall—
  Its power departed, fame, and glory!

No hand removes the gathered rust with friendly care;
  No voice speaks now in tones caressing;
No soul of burning faith, before the dawn at prayer,
  Repeats the graven holy blessing. . . .

And thus it is with you, O poet, who have flung away
    In our complaisant generation
Your mission in the world, exchanged for gold your sway
    Over crowds mute with adoration.

Time was when, resolute, your ringing words inflamed
    The warriors with fierce emotion,
When they were needful, as wine at a feast acclaimed,
    As myrrh and incense for devotion.

On multitudes your brave impassioned message fell,
    Inspired by thought and noble feeling,
A godlike voice, resounding far as a folkmoot bell
    A people's joy or danger pealing.

Today they find delight in pomp and shameful lies.
    They mock your words sublime and human!
They rouge their aged fears, their creeping rot disguise,
    A world grown old, a sickened woman!

O prophet mocked! When will your ringing words arouse
    Mankind again? Or will you never
Pluck out your ancient sword, avenger swift, but drowse
    Concealed in rust and shame forever?

1838

O Dreamer, Disbelieve Your Dream

O Dreamer, disbelieve the rapture of your dream,
    And fear as bane your inspiration!
Your troubled mood is but the soul's disease, the theme
    Of captive thought in agitation;
No sign of godlike favor, it is your blood at strife,
    Your spirit's fulness of emotion.
Then hasten day after day in common cares of life
    To drain away that baneful potion!

And if, by chance, revealed upon some magic hour,
    In the deep of your spirit hidden,
A new unfathomable fountain-source of power
    Arises with pure sounds unbidden,
O do not yield to their enchantment! Let them stay
    In dark forgetfulness unspoken:
Your measured and unfeeling verses will betray
    Their depths of harmony unbroken.

And should your spirit grieve alone with secret grace,
    In thunder, wind, by love attended,
Then do not rush into the brawling market-place
    With cries of wrath uncomprehended.
Be great, ashamed to trade in grief or wrath, to hear
    The crowds about your sorrows babble,
Ashamed to make a boastful show of hurt and fear
    Before the simple-minded rabble!

Not their concern to know your sorrows and your fears,
    The reason for your grief and passion,

Or hear what idle hopes you mused in boyhood years
    And why your anger and compassion!
Behold the mirthful crowds, sauntering here and there,
    Who do not look before or after—
No trace, as is befitting them, of tears and care
    To mar their faces gay with laughter!

And yet among the poorest there you'd rarely meet
    A man who seems—unless by crime
And misery defiled, or ravaged by defeat,—
    Worn out by grief before his time.
Believe, they are amused by your reproof and rage,
    Your old refrains and older craving,
As by a painted actor come upon the stage,
    In wrath a sword of cardboard waving.

1839

Three Palms
(A Legend of the East)

In days long ago in Arabia's land
Three palms stood majestic and tall on the sand;
A fountain that rose from the desolate ground
Played sparkling between with murmuring sound,
In shade of green leaves protected at noon
From the blaze of sun and the breath of simoon.

And year after year in silence went by.
From out of the desert no pilgrim came nigh
The oasis to quiet the pain in his breast,
To drink of the spring, in the shadow to rest.
The leaves and the fountain with murmuring sweet
Began to decay and to shrink in the heat.

Then cried in complaint the palms unto God:
"Oh, cruel our fate! by the scourge of Thy rod
We droop in the desert, doomed to defeat;
We are shaken by storms and wasted by heat,
And, giving no pleasure to others, we die!
Our fate is unjust, O great ruler on high!"

They ceased, when lo! in a haze of blue light
The sands rose in columns of gold in their sight;
With burdens and carpets bright in the sun
And tinkling of silvery bells, one by one,
Soon camel on camel came swaying in motion,
Like shallops arising upon a blue ocean.

The motley tents of the nomads rose high
On the humps of the camels, and often a shy
Impatient dark hand moved the curtains about,
And glowing black eyes on the desert peered out.
Bent low in his saddle, the Arab in haste
Across the great desert triumphantly raced.

And rearing and prancing, his horse on the plain
Sprang forth like a panther the hunter has slain;
The flowing burnoose, like a banner all fair,
From the Islamite's shoulders flapped in the air,
As, shouting in joy, he raced on the ground,
Hurling and catching his spear at a bound.

Then soon to the palms came the caravan near,
And under their shadows the camp rang with cheer.
They lowered their gourds in the waters aglow,
And rejoicing to welcome the pilgrims below,
The murmuring leaves waved long in their pride;
The fountain sang soft in the cool eventide.

When darkness had covered the desert in calm,
They struck with an axe at the base of each palm,
And lifeless the heirs of the ages fell down!
With laughter the children plundered each crown;
The trunks were cut; they were broken and torn.
And slowly they burned in the fire till morn.

As the shadows departed before the new day,
The caravan rose and journeyed away;
The cold grey cinders and ashes alone

Remained on the sands where the fountain shone;
The fiery sun burned the shrivelled remains;
The whirlwind scattered them over the plains.

And now, in stillness, in loneliness dread,
No longer the spring hears the leaves overhead.
And vainly it cries unto Allah its prayer
For shelter and shade in the sands, in despair;
The vultures alone in the wilderness wing,
And devour their prey near the desolate spring.

1839

Prayer

When care and sorrow hover
Within my gloomy hour,
I pray, repeating over,
A prayer of wondrous power.

In sounds of adoration,
In words of holiness,
I find true consolation
And secret loveliness.

All fear and all misgiving
Then leave me in the night:
I arise, in tears, believing,
And, oh, my heart is light!

1839

The Gifts of Terek

Terek rages, wild and angry,
Through the mountains on his way;
Like a tempest rings his wailing
In his gleaming tears of spray.
Then he flows along the level
Lowland, gliding craftily,
With a meek caressing murmur
Greeting low the Caspian Sea:

"Oh, receive me, ancient ocean!
Shelter me within thy breast!
I have wandered long in freedom;
It is time for me to rest.
I was born on Mount Kazbék
Where the white clouds gave me suck,
And against mankind's invasion
In my hate I ever struck.
Always, to delight thy children,
Daryal Pass in wrath I tore,
And my gift of stones and boulders
For their games I hither bore."

On the shore reclining, peaceful,
As in sleep the Caspian lay.
But again with tender greeting
Terek thus began to pray:

"Hear, I bear to thee a present,
Not a common offering!

From the battlefield the bravest
Chief of Kabardin I bring!
He is clad in priceless armor,
And the gauntlet on his hand
Bears in gold a Koran blessing
Given in the Holy Land.
Stern his brows are drawn together,
Pale his countenance and seared,
And his noble blood lies clotted
Dark upon his flowing beard.
From his open eyes the ancient
Hatreds born of warfare glare;
Down his neck upon the billows
Flows his matted raven hair."

In a dream the Caspian, silent,
Lay upon the long white shore.
And the angry Terek, tossing,
Spoke unto the sea once more:

"Father, hear me! yet the fairest
Gift above all gifts I hide,
Guarded safely in my bosom
From the world within my tide.
A fair Cossak maiden shrouded
Deep within my waves I bear,—
Beautiful her gleaming shoulders
And like gold her flowing hair.
Softly still her face in sadness,
Softly still her eyes in rest,
While the crimson blood is flowing
From a wound upon her breast.

One brave lad among the bravest
Perished for his love unwed;
One alone in all the hamlets
Grieves no longer for the dead:
In his last despair and sorrow,
In a bloody midnight strife
With a Chechen chief in combat
He had flung away his life."

Terek ceased, the angry river.
Then as white as driven snows,
A pale face and tresses golden
Swaying on the billows rose.

The grey sea awoke in splendor;
Loud his thunder in the skies;
And a mist of tender passion
Hung upon his dark blue eyes.
The grey sea arose in gladness,
In his splendor, in his might,
And the waves of Terek greeted
With a murmur of delight.

1839

In Memory of Alexander Odóyevsky

I knew him well. We roamed together, fast
In friendship, in the mountains of the East,
And there in loneliness of exile passed
Our days. When from my sufferings released,
I came to native fields and home. In vain
His hope for freedom from his banishment.
Death cut him down inside a soldier's tent,
Where, sick in body but untamed, in pain
He died.—None holds him now. His dreams are slain,
His winging words and youthful fantasies,
His hopes deceived and bitter memories.

It was for those bright hopes that he was born,
For joy, for poetry. But, wild with strife,
Too soon his boyhood bonds he tore with scorn,
And flung his heart into the sea of life,
By God and man rejected. Yet in our night
Of ruthless dark, by toil and grief surrounded,
By men's confusion, or by deserts bounded,
His quiet flame, undimmed, kept burning white:
Ah, sacred soul! his azure eyes of light,
His boyish laughter and his living mind,
His noble faith in life for all mankind!

He is dead, my Sasha! Far from home he perished,
One whom the great had hunted. Sleep apart
Deep in an alien land! In friendship cherished,
Dream softly as my love within my heart
Deep-buried dreams, your lonely name enshrining.

You died, as many die, unknown to fame,
Resigned and strong of heart. The secret flame
Of thought upon your forehead brightly shining,
Your soul departed, with the sun declining;
Your words, as life went out, in likelihood
They heard, but none their meaning understood.

What was your sense from word to word? A sigh
For passing youth, a greeting home, the throes
Of ebbing life at death, or but a cry
For some remembered friend or dream?—Who knows?
Their bitter meaning and the depth and grace
Of those soft words you spoke, the last to fall,
Are lost.... The matter, aim, belief, and all
Your thoughts have vanished now without a trace,
Like vapors of the air in empty space
That in the sky a golden moment gleam
And soon are blown: Whence, where, and why our dream?

As a cloud that never leaves a trace behind,
Or as the fleeting passion of a child,
Faded in air his dream, faded his mind,
And with his truth he died, unreconciled.
What matter? Let the world forget this brave
Man's life so strangely beautiful and pure.
What use their empty calumnies, their lure
Of praise and fame to him who was no slave
Of time, who scorned the world unto his grave
And cast aside its subtle slavish chains? ...
He loved the sea, the silence of the plains.

He loved the mountain peaks in snow and rain.
About his grave unknown, the earth and sea,
His everlasting friends, on guard remain
United in their wondrous destiny.
The plain lies vast and blue in silence sealed;
With silver crown the Caucasus around
Looms, frowning, in a mist of dream and sound,
Like some great giant leaning on his shield
Who hears the roving waters rise with song
While the Black Sea resounding thunders long.

1839

Prince Alexander Ivanovich Odoyevsky (1802-1839) was a minor poet. He took part in the Decembrist Revolt in 1825; he was sentenced to hard labor in Siberia, then transferred to the Caucasus in 1837. He was stationed at the Lazarevsk fortress where nearly half of the regiment perished from scurvy and malaria. Odoyevsky died on 15 August, 1839. His poem, in answer to Pushkin's message to friends in Siberia, won him a permanent place in Russian poetry and social history. The line, "the spark will burst into a flame," became the watch-word of Lenin's newspaper *Iskra* (The Spark), founded in 1900.

New Year's Night

How oft, surrounded by a gay and festive crowd,
When round me interweave as in a dreamy cloud
    Their din of music and the dance,
And hum of polished empty talk; when figures glide
Before me like soulless forms upon a ghostly tide,
    In masks of formal elegance;

Or when with artful unconcern and self-command,
The ballroom beauties brush my unresponsive hand
    With fingers long unmoved by fear,—
Though sharing outwardly in all their show and glare,
I cherish in my lonely heart an image fair
    And hallowed of a bygone year.

And if by chance I can forget the life that weighs
Me down, I fly to days so sad, so strange—my days
    Of old so wonderfully new!
I see myself a child at home, and I behold
The ruined garden lanes, the lofty manor old,
    The flower beds in evening dew.

I see the sleepy pond all mantled with green weeds,
The smoke from clustered village huts, and in the meads
    The mist arising far aloft.
I come into a gloomy garden lane; the red
Sky gleams within the trees, and neath my timid tread
    The gold leaves, yielding, rustle soft.

I feel a strange and heavy yearning in my breast.
I weep with thinking of my dream—my perfect, best,
    True worship of a dream of love
So real to me—my dream of radiant blue eyes
And rosy smile of sweetness kindling as the skies
    Of early dawn behind the grove.

Thus in my wonderland, lord of my great domain,
I live uncounted hours alone. Their still refrain
    Lives trembling in my memory
Amid the troubled storms of passion and of doubt,
Like some green solitary island, safe, far out,
    Smiling upon a desert sea.

But when I wake and know again the mocking gleam,
And when the noise of revellers affrights my dream,
    My gentle uninvited guest,—
Then wild I long to stun them in their mirth, to fling
At them the challenge of my iron verse with sting
    And wrathful fury of my breast!

1840

I am Lonely and Sad

I am lonely and sad. In the hour of trial and pain
    Not a friend to whom I may go.
Have wishes a meaning if wishes are always in vain,
    While years go by, the fairest I know?

To love,—but whom? It is idle to love for a day,
    And love will cease on the morrow.
I look in my heart: Of the past it has nothing to say
    And nothing of gladness or sorrow.

What use a great passion, a rapture that suddenly dies,
    By reason defeated? At best,
This life, as I scan it with open unprejudiced eyes,
    Seems an empty, wearisome jest.

1840

Cossack Cradlesong

Hush, my darling, time for sleeping,
    Hush, my baby, do!
For the watchful moon is shining
    In the sky for you.
I will tell you ancient stories,
    Sing a song for you;
Only close your eyes in slumber,
    Hush, my baby, do!

Terek flows among the mountains
    With a roaring sound;
In the night the evil Chechen
    Steals along the ground.
But your father's old in battle,
    And in warfare true:
Sleep, my darling, sleep in quiet,
    Hush, my baby, do!

You will learn the ways of fighting
    For your fatherland,
Like a fearless horseman faring,
    With your gun in hand.
Then your saddle-cloth in rarest
    Threads of silk I'll do.
Sleep, my darling, sleep in quiet,
    Hush, my baby, do!

You will be a stalwart Cossack
    Who will never yield;

I will come to see you leaving
    For the battlefield.
Many tears I will in sadness
    Weep at night for you!
Slumber sweet, my shining angel,
    Hush, my baby, do!

I will languish sad and lonely,
    Waiting wearily
Day by day in faith and prayer
    Till you come to me.
I will fear that you are pining,
    Sad and lonely too.
Sleep while free of care and trouble,
    Hush, my baby, do!

You will have your mother's icon
    When you ride away.
Kneel before the holy image
    When to God you pray.
Hold me always closer, always
    In remembrance true:
Hush, my darling, time for sleeping,
    Hush, my baby, do!

1840

The Captive Knight

Silent I gaze through the bars of my prison,
Watching, in sadness, the sky aglow.
Far in the blue I can see the birds flying;
Weary, I sigh in my shame, in my woe.

Still are my lips; I have never a prayer,
Never a song, in praise of my love:
Only the battles of old I remember,
Only my sword, my helmet, and glove.

Now in this armor of granite I languish,
Now on my forehead the helmet is stone;
Safe is my shield from lances and arrows;
Free in the meadow, my steed runs alone.

Time is my steed—he is swift and unfailing;
Bars in the window—my visor of yore;
Stronger than armor the walls of my prison,
Stronger than shields the fast iron door.

Faint, in this armor, I lie in my prison.
Swifter, O Time, be swifter in flight!
Death, at the last, will hold up my stirrup;
Raising my visor, I will soon alight.

1840

Wherefore

I grieve because I love, and, loving you,
I know their crafty rumors will pursue
Your youth in flower, lying out of spite.
For every shining hour and true delight
Fate will demand in hurt and tears its pay.
I grieve—because you are so free and gay.

1840

Gratitude

For all, for all Thou sendest I am grateful:
For secret pangs of passion and my woes,
For tears too bitter and for kisses hateful,
For spite of friends, and vengeance of my foes;
For all my baffled dreams that cheated me,
For all my ardor wasted, all my grief!—
But make it so, for all Thy gifts to me,
My days of thankfulness be very brief.

1840

Mountain Heights
(after Goethe)

Mountain heights are sleeping
Now in evening light;
Mists are softly creeping
Down the vales of night.
The road's dark and lonely;
Peace in leaf and tree....
Wait a moment only:
Peace will come to thee.

1840

The poem is a free translation of Goethe's *Ueber allen Gipfeln ist Ruh*. Lermontov paraphrased the lines "Warte nur, balde ruhest du auch" in such a way as to suggest eternal rest and immortality. His death-wish flared up in the ironical *Gratitude*, in *Testament*, and in *Lone I Walk at Night*.

Lines to a Child

Once more the anguish of my youth I dream,
And trembling with some happiness supreme
And inner fear, I look at you, dear child.
I wish you understood today how wild
My heart, how great my tender secrecy,
How dear your laughter and your gaiety,
How sweet your lively eyes, your golden hair,
Your voice! ... I know, like hers, how truly fair
Your ways! Long years, alas, of grief and pain
Have changed her life, but in my heart remain
The air divine, the dream, the light I knew
Within her eyes. . . . But you, you love me true?
Or do I weary you? Do I surprise,
Caressing you? too often kiss your eyes?
Or warm upon your cheeks my burning tears?—
No, darling, not a word about my fears
And grief to her, and not a word of me!
Your childish talk may rouse uneasily
Her anger. . . . Trust me always! When at night,
In kneeling down before the taper light,
Close by your bed, she whispered soft and low,
Endearing names repeating, names you know,
And formed your fingers in a cross to pray
Together, did she ask you then to say
Another name, to pray for one name more?
In a low whisper, paler than before,
Did she speak a name you have forgotten?—**No**.
No matter, child! A name's at best, I know,

An empty sound! May heaven ever keep
That name unknown. But should it some day leap
To mind, somewhere, branded by men with shame,
Recall your childhood and do not curse that name!

1840

To A. O. Smirnóva

When absent, I have much to say,
But crave your voice alone when near:
So stern your eyes, I turn away,
Confused, in silence and in fear.
I do not hope to reach your mind,
Or touch with artless words your heart.
It seems amusing, but I find
Defeat and grief my fated part.

1840

To a Portrait

At times like a frolicsome tomboy,
At times like a butterfly gay,
In words unaffected and simple
The homeliest greeting you say.

Impulsive your manner of pleasing,
And custom you brook as a snare;
You're swift as a snake in the grasses,
And swift as a bird in the air.

Your innocent nature, in secret,
Now gladness, now sorrow denies:
As dark as the deep of the ocean
Your soul; the clear sky, in your eyes.

The truth for a moment your fashion,
Then feigning and falsehood your use!
'Tis hard, I am sure, to know you;
It is harder my love to refuse.

1840

Clouds

Hear me, O clouds eternally wandering,
Fleeing in azure, your pearly wings riven,
Fleeing like me, dear fellowship sundering,
Far to the south into banishment driven!

Why are you driven, by whom? By insensible
Slander, in secret, or openly hated?
Hounded by enemies? or, indefensible,
Are you then branded by crime unabated?

No, you're fleeing bare fields in their weariness!
Feeling no passion, no sorrow, or punishment,
Homeless you wander, in freedom, in dreariness.
Ah, no country can doom you to banishment.

1840

Farewell to Russia

Land of the unwashed, goodbye!
Land of masters, land of knaves!
You, in neat blue uniforms!
You who live like cringing slaves!

In my exile I may find
Peace beneath Caucasian skies,—
Far from slanderers and tsars,
Far from ever-spying eyes.

1840

Valerik

    I write to you—by chance. I hardly know
The reason why I do. I've lost that right.
Indeed, what could I say to you? To urge
I've not forgotten you? You know it long;
Besides, it really makes no difference now.

    You wouldn't care to know my way of life,
Our far-off wilds. In spirit we are far
Apart; I doubt two beings anywhere
Can be as one in life. I have with care,
Unprejudiced, reflected on the past
And fear in every way I'm losing faith.
It's ludicrous to play the hypocrite
And make a show of cheer, or fool myself.
And what the gain to keep believing things
No longer true? To dream of some great love?
Today love's for the hour, a thing apart.
And yet I think of you, no matter what.

    I never will forget you. Why? Because
I loved you very much and long; then, too,
Because I've paid with suffering and fear
For every drop of happiness I got,
Because, in fact, despite my vain regret,
I have endured the chains of heavy years
And killed the bloom of life with cold reflection.
I had no ease in meeting friends, and thus
Youth passed me by—its fun, romance, and love.
But you, of all the world, I can't forget.

I've come to think by now it is my fate
To bear my cross with patience and accept
My punishment.   I'm older and much wiser.
I thank the stars for every good or ill
That comes my way, as Orientals do,
And ask for nothing more. I suffer wrong
In silence, and think perhaps the East itself,
Without my knowing it, bestowed on me
Her deeper mood. Perhaps by constant toil
And cares, by being always on the move
With little time for thought, I'm closer here
To nature. In any case, my soul's asleep,
My fancy cribbed, my mind without a care.
I sprawl at ease on grass and dream beneath
The shadow of the plane tree and the vine,
While all about me gleam the soldiers' tents.

    The Cossack horses, huddled, stand in rows
With lowered heads; the men lie dozing by
The cannon-pieces; low, the smoking wicks.
With bayonets bright gleaming in the sun,
Afar our soldiers stand on guard in pairs.
I hear men talking of old times inside
A tent: how they campaigned with Yermolóv
Across the mountain ranges; how they fought
And won or lost in wars against the natives.
Behind the tents, beside the stream a Tartar
Devoutly prays according to his faith,
Alone, while others in a circle chat.
I like their row of yellow-shining faces,
Their caps, their narrow sleeves around the elbows,
Their sly dark glances, and their throaty talk.

A sudden shot rings out afar; a bullet
Flies whizzing in the air; then someone shouts
And silence falls again.... The heat goes down;
The infantry's astir; it's time to water
The horses now. One rider, then another
Shoots by; the camp grows noisier with talk:
Where is the second squad? Is it packing time?
And where's the captain? Get the wagons out!
Hey, buddy, lend a light!—The drums are beating;
The band is droning loud; the guns are rattling
Between the marching ranks. And to the front
A general rides forward with his staff.

Like bees the Cossacks scatter in the fields
With yells, their banners skirting now the woods.
A turbaned Moslem in a crimson mantle
Rides bravely on his prancing spotted horse,
And dares our men, the madcap, to a fight.
And, lo! a Cossack gamely flies to meet him,
With gun in hand. The hoofs of horses, smoke,
And flying shots. Who's wounded? Well, no matter!
And hotter grows the crossfire all around.

There's much of daring sport but little meaning
In these high-hearted bouts. We often watched
Them in the cool late afternoons, amused,
Without excitement, like a lively play
At home; and yet I also witnessed games
Too wild and bloody for a tragic play.

At Ghikh, for instance, once we made our way
Through thickest woods; the clear-blue sky above

Was like a vaulted roof on fire. We knew
That a battle lay ahead, that native hordes
From mountain hamlets in their common cause
Were gathering in Chechen lands. We glimpsed
Their signal towers above the forest tops
In columns and low-lying clouds of smoke.
The woods soon grew alive with savage calls
Reverberating in the forest fastness.
Our baggage train had scarce come in the open
When the fight began. The rear-guard called for help.
Some brought up guns; some bore the wounded out
And called to doctors. From the woods at left
The enemy rushed upon our guns with yells
And hail of bullets from behind the trees.
Ahead, the place was still; a stream ran through
The underbrush. Nearer we came and hurled
Some shells; we edged still nearer; nothing stirred.
Then bright behind a pile of trunks we saw
A glint of steel, a cap or two perhaps,
Soon hidden deep in grass. The air was dread
With silence; one brief while and every heart
Beat fast in fearful secret expectation.
One volley rang—we saw their rows in grass!
Not waiting long—our men were tough old hands
In war—we cried: To bayonets! We stormed,
Our officers in front, with hearts aflame;
On horseback some against the ramparts flew,
But most on foot. With daggers, butts of guns,
We slaughtered; hand to hand for full two hours
The battle lasted, fought in trench and stream.
We killed in silence breast to breast, like beasts
In fury; piles of bodies choked the stream.

I tried, because of heat and weariness,
To drink,—the stream was muddied, warm, and red.

   Beneath an oak tree, near the shore, a pace
Or so behind the line of ramparts, stood
A silent group, one soldier on his knees.
They looked like hard and gloomy men at first,
But tears ran slowly down their faces dark
With dust. Against the oak their captain lay
With two black wounds upon his breast; the blood
Ran ebbing slowly drop by drop; his breath
Came hard; his eyes grew wild and wandering.
His whispers begged them to save the general
Whom he dreamed surrounded in a fight, alone.
Thus long he moaned, but slowly weaker grew,
And soon his life went out. Old soldiers steeled
In long campaigns, then leaning on their guns,
In silence wept. They wrapped a mantle round
His body, and with care they carried him to
His lonely grave. As if rooted to the ground
I stood and watched their going, deep in grief.
I heard as men around me with a sigh
Spoke gently of their fallen friends, and yet
I felt no real compassion in my heart.

   The field lay still, dead bodies in a pile;
The blood was dripping, smoking on the ground,
And filled the air with heavy reeking fumes.
In shade one general sat astride a drum
And listened to reports. The woods around
Shone blue as in a mist with battle smoke,
But far away the chain of mountains rose

With peaks eternal in their pride and peace.
There shone in light celestial Mount Kazbek.
And in my heart with secret grief I mused
How poor a thing is man: What does he want?
The sky is bright, and there is room enough
For all on earth; yet endlessly, in vain,
Alone he lives in strife and hatred. Why?
Haroun, who was my native friend, cut short
My dreaming with a slap across my back.
I asked what name the stream had here among
His people. "Valerík," he said. It means,
Translated in our tongue, the stream of death,
A name it bore with men of ancient days.
"How many, do you think, have fought today?"
"Some seven thousand." "Were their losses great?"
"Who knows? You should have counted them yourself."
But here another voice broke in to say
They won't too soon forget that bloody day.
My Chechen friend looked craftily at me,
But only shook his head, and said no more.

    I think I'm boring you. The anxieties
Of war seem droll among the worldly great
At home. You are not often vexed in mind
About the means and ends of our existence,
And there is not a trace of care or grief
In you, because you do not know in fact
How people die. God spare you then the truth
Of war; we have enough of other cares.
'Tis better far to die in peace and love,
To sleep the everlasting sleep of life
At last, and dream the day of resurrection.

And now, goodbye! And if my simple story
Can bring a bit of happiness to you,
I shall be happy too. If not, I hope
You will forgive my tale as but a prank,
And whisper softly: Why, the fellow's queer!

1840

Lermontov was exiled to the Caucasus for a second time in May 1840. He was assigned to the Grozny fortress in the Chechen region, a dangerous front under constant attack by native tribes. At the river Valerik a bloody engagement took place on 11 July. The poet distinguished himself in all combats. He was cited for bravery and leadership but Tsar Nicholas refused to sanction the decorations recommended by the military staffs. (The poem is iambic tetrameter in form, rhymed, but it seemed best to render this poetic letter in blank verse).

Valerik is a miracle of stark realism in literature, objective in all details. The Caucasus was the scene of Lermontov's poetic growth and life,— and the scene of his death in a duel. Tsar Nicholas and his henchmen desired such an end for the young officer who hated them as hangmen of Freedom and as the real murderers of Pushkin.

The Testament

I want to be alone with you
A little while, my friend:
It can't be long; my days are few
To live, and soon the end.
I see you're going home on leave.
Then listen ... no! I do believe
There's no one over there
Who'll ask for me, or care.

And yet if someone asks—one might,
It doesn't matter who,—
Say a bullet hit me in the fight
And that I'm really through.
Explain how poor our doctors are
And that I served in faith the tsar;
And do remember me
To friends I'll never see.

I don't imagine you will find
My folks are living now. . . .
I'd really suffer in my mind
To grieve them anyhow.
But if by chance they live, then say
I'm poor at writing, far away;
They must not wait in vain
My coming home again.

We had a neighbor there nearby.
How very long ago,

Come think of it, we said goodbye!
She'll never ask, I know....
But tell her everything, apart,
And do not spare her empty heart:
She'll cry a little . . . let her—
To her it doesn't matter!

1840

Vindication

When nothing but their spiteful rumors
About my erring ways and shame
Remain remembered in the world
As wrongs dishonoring my name;

When in a grave unknown will slumber
My heart that panted deep with pain,
My dreaming heart where passion splendid
And hatred struggled long in vain;

And when with drooping head, in silence,
You hear their judgment and their blame,
And your unspotted life of perfect
Love should become your doom and shame;

For him, whose passion and offences
Have darkened all your days of youth,
I pray, forbear in your reproaches
To speak his name with stinging truth.

Before the bar of crafty judges
Say that another Judge is King,
And that the right of true forgiveness
You purchased with your suffering.

1841

My Native Land

I love my country, but my love is strange
And rare, a love that reason cannot change.
It is not my country's victories, nor fame
So dearly bought with blood, nor ancient claim
Of rich tradition, glory, and command
That stir sweet reveries about my native land.

Not these bring quiet joy. I love—I know
Not why—her rivers at the flood like seas,
The voices of her boundless forest trees,
The frozen silence of her plains in snow.
I love to ride for days inside a jolting cart
On dusty lanes, and, searching slow the evening shadows,
To dream of lodgings near and hail with thankful heart
A blur of trembling village light among the meadows.

> I love the smell of stubble burning,
> The wagons huddled on the plain
> At night, a pair of silver birches
> Above a field of yellow grain.
> With gladness few can share, I see
> The grain upon the threshing floor,
> The lowly cottage with its trim
> Above the window and the door.
> I'm glad to watch on holidays
> The stamp of dancers on the ground,
> And hear until the morning's near
> The talk of tipsy peasants round.

1841

A Dead Man's Love

My body, it is true, lies buried
    Deep in a grave,
Yet everywhere forever, dearest,
    Your love I crave.
Beyond the earth, in highest regions
    Of bliss above,
I still remember all my anguish
    And pangs of love.

I hoped, at death, our earthly parting—
    An end to pain,
And peace at last forevermore;
    I hoped in vain.
I saw the pure unbodied spirits,
    But longed for you;
I sought, in grief, among the blessed
    Your features true.

What bliss to me celestial glory,
    And paradise,
When still I suffer earthly passions
    And earthly sighs?
When dearer than the bliss of Heaven
    Your love I hold;
When still I yearn with jealous weeping
    As in days of old?

I long, I tremble, dear! My hope
    Within me dies,

Lest another with endearment gazes
    Into your eyes.
And if you whisper in your slumber
    Another name,
Your words would make my spirit wither
    As in a flame.

You shall not love another, never!
    O love divine!
By sacred words and pledges spoken
    You are wholly mine.
What meaning all your fear and prayer
    Beside the grave?
Not peace, oblivion, nor bliss
    For myself I crave!

1841

Agreement

Let idle crowds defame, disdainful,
Your love they cannot know nor guess,
And then through scorn and prejudice
Deny your bonds of tenderness.

No slave unto the world's opinion,
I do not kneel before the great;
Like you, I think their cause unworthy
My heart's devotion or my hate.

Like you, I share their noisy pleasures,
Yet know them not as souls apart:
I take alike the wise and foolish
And keep the mandate of my heart.

Alike, we do not prize their world,
Their happiness, their ways. We say
We never can betray each other,
Nor strangers you or me betray.

So brief the time for meeting now
As friends when we must part again,
And so unreal our happiness,
We part with little grief or pain.

1841

The Cliff

A golden cloud at evening came
To sleep upon the mountain's breast.
And, gay, at dawn she left the crest
To wander in the sky, aflame.

A trace of dew, of night's caress,
Remained upon his ancient face of stone.
He looms as in a dream, alone,
And softly weeps within the wilderness.

1841

The Dispute

Once more among the mountains
    Of the Caucasus
Between Kazbèk and Elbrus
    A quarrel rose.
"Take care, my friend Kazbèk!"
    Grey Elbrus cried:
"You will regret your yielding
    To the human tide.
They'll build their smoky hovels
    On your mountainside,
And the axe will ring, resounding
    In your gorges wide.
With swinging pick and shovel
    They'll cut deep roads
To your stony heart for copper
    And the golden lodes.
Their caravans already
    To your summits steal,
Where clouds alone are climbing,
    Where eagles wheel.
Man is shrewd, and though he loses
    His first swift fight,
Take care! The East is teeming,
    Waxing great in might!"

"Why fear the East?" Kazbèk
    At the warning jeers;
"There man has lain in slumber
    Nine hundred years.

Behold the sleepy Gruzian
    In the plane-tree shade,
While honeyed wine is running
    On his silk brocade!
And there, in smoke of nargile,
    On a rich divan,
Under jewel-gleaming fountains,
    In a dream, Teheran!
To the gates of Zion, wasted
    By Jehovah's hand,
A graveyard still and voiceless,
    The Judean land;
And beyond, in torrid noonday,
    The slow-moving waves
Of the yellow Nile are laving
    The ancient graves.
The wild Bedouin has forgotten
    His raids and steeds,
And sings in his tents the glory
    Of his fathers' deeds.
The East lies deep in slumber,
    All at ease, unfree!
No feeble East will conquer
    Or master me!"

"Do not boast too soon," said Elbrus;
    "Lift up your eyes
And behold the moving shadows
    Under northern skies!"

In confusion then Kazbèk,
    In his dark amaze,

In deep silence to the northward
    Turned a troubled gaze.
He looked afar in wonder,
    In fear profound;
He beheld a strange commotion,
    Heard a tramping sound:
From the Ural to the Danube,
    To the river's course,
In dancing sunlight gleaming
    Moved a mighty force.
He beheld the banners waving
    Like a field of grass,
And, in clouds of dust, battalions
    Of the Uhlans pass.
He beheld the swarming armies
    By divisions come;
Before them moved the standards,
    Boomed the martial drum.
Then the batteries came crashing
    With clanging might,
With their cannon torches ready
    As before a fight.
Like an eagle, firm in power,
    Tried in battles won,
A commander old in warfare
    Led his soldiers on.
They came, the surging armies,
    Like a torrent loud,
Like a fearful storm descending
    In a thunder-cloud....

And oppressed by dread and anguish
    Kazbèk, in gloom, arose

His great enemies to number,
　　His uncounted foes.
He beheld the peaks in sadness,
　　His friends of old,
And drew down his snowy turban
　　In eternal cold.

1841

A Dream

I dreamed that in a vale of Daghestan,
With a bullet in my breast, alone I lay,
That from a smoking wound my lifeblood ran
Into the sands,—ran drop by drop away.

I lay upon the valley floor, alone
On desert sands beneath a craggy steep;
The sun burned on the yellow peaks, and shone
Upon me too, but lifeless was my sleep.

I dreamed I was at home on holiday
And saw a banquet room with lights aflame;
I saw fair women garlanded and gay
And heard them speak light-heartedly my name.

But one as in a dream sat lone, apart,
Not joining in their round of gaiety:
God knows what secret fancy made her heart
Grow sad or why she seemed to dream of me.

She dreamed she saw the vale of Daghestan
And knew that, lifeless, in the sun I lay,
As from a black deep wound my blood still ran
On desert sands,—ran drop by drop away.

1841

Tamára

In the narrow deep of Daryál
Where Terek writhes in gloom,
Once rose a lonely old tower
On a drear, dark cliff of doom.

Long ago in that desolate tower
There lived Tamára the queen:
She lived like a demon in evil;
She moved like an angel serene.

There glittered in mist at midnight
A golden mysterious light,
The heart of the pilgrim alluring
With promise of rest in the night.

At night rang the voice of Tamára;
It quivered with passion and pain,
Descending with witching enchantment
And spell of a luring refrain.

Then warrior, trader, or herdsman
Came out from the night at her call.
A portal swung open; a eunuch
Saluted the guest in the hall.

In jewels, on cushions of velvet,
Adorned as a princess divine,
Tamára lay waiting,—before her,
Two goblets of hissing red wine.

With rapture and trembling caresses
And clasping of hands in delight,
Their outcries of passion and revel
Divided the darkness of night,

As though in that desolate tower
A hundred mad lovers made feast
At a bridal, or honored the passing
Of a sovereign king of the East.

But scarce a sunray of morning
Awakened mountain and plain
When silence and deep desolation
Enfolded the tower again.

And only the turbulent Terek
Disputed the silence profound;
His waves sprang higher in fury
And raced with a thunderous sound.

They bore in their waters a body
And hastened with wailing and cries;
A hand shone white at a casement
In a farewell murmur of sighs.

So tender the murmur of parting
And sweet with languishing pain,
It seemed a pledge of their meeting
And of love and caresses again.

1841

The Rendezvous

Behind the purpling evening
    The mountain ranges dream,
And softly in the shadows
    Flashes the silver stream.
The flowers fill each garden
    Awake with sweetness new;
Tiflís is wrapped in silence,
    Ravines in dimness blue.
Now dreams of evil hover
    Above the sinners' heads,
And angels speak with children
    Asleep in quiet beds.

Above the cliff, in darkness,
    A castle rises high;
Close by beneath a plane tree
    On woven rugs I lie.
Alone I lie and wonder:
    In truth or mockery
Did you promise in the evening
    To keep a tryst with me?
In this hour of secret being,
    Of love and sweet delight,
I call you best and faithful
    Within the gloomy night.

Along the bridge below me
    Rise points of light aglow;
Black towers loom in darkness
    Like watchmen in a row.

From all the watering places
    I see on every side,
In robes of white, like shadows
    The Gruzian women glide.
In silent pairs, in darkness,
    They move along the trails;
But I do not find your likeness
    Among the flowing veils.

Your little house and terrace
    I now can see from far,
The porch and steps reflected
    Within the shallow bar.
Beside the Kura, mantled
    In coolness and in blue,
It stands enclosed with ivy
    And flower beds in dew.
I see behind a poplar
    A window in the wall:
But where the lamp you promised
    To light at evenfall?

I wait with deep misgiving;
    I watch in vain your hut;
Impatient, with my dagger
    The woven rug I cut.
I wait alone, in anguish,
    And heavy is my heart;
The night grows colder, paler,
    And shadows move apart.
In amber light emerges
    Afar a mountain crest;

The caravans of camels
    Awaken from their rest.

Forget her love and promise!
    O soul of wrath, awake!
I know she is unfaithful,
    A mocker and a snake!
I know full well the reason
    Why on the ringing way
A Tartar youth came riding
    In a hurry yesterday.
He rode beneath her window,
    His Persian steed astride;
Her father shrewdly prizes
    The steed he rode in pride.

I'll take my trusty rifle
    And go across the vale;
I know a craggy hillside,
    I know a narrow trail.
Alone, I will be waiting,
    Alone on watch remain;
I will cover with my rifle
    The hill and dusty plain.
Be strong, O heart, be patient!
    I crouch beside a stone.
Who gallops in the mountains?
    My rival,—and alone.

1841

An Oak Leaf

One leaf of the oak from his branch tore away,
And, lashed by a storm, he wandered astray;
All withered by heat and the wintery blast,
He fell on the shore of the Black Sea at last.

The fairest chinar grew tall near the sea;
The breezes caressed the green leaves of the tree;
The birds sang in rapture, their feathers in flame;
They told of a mermaid, they fluted her name.

The pilgrim lay near the chinar in his grief,
Imploring cool rest for a day and relief.
Behold me!—he prayed—in my desolate North
I grew up too soon, and too soon came forth.

Alone, without aim, I wandered on earth;
I am faint and withered from weather and dearth.
O let me remain with your leaves for a day!
I will tell them of wonders I heard on my way.

Of what good are you,—the chinar then replied,—
All yellow and dry, with my children to bide?
What profit your stories? With strains of their song
The birds in my branches have tired me long.

Go, pilgrim, your way! Your breed is not mine!
I'm loved by the sun; in its glory I shine.
My branches I lift to the sky in my pride,
And my roots are washed by the great sea tide.

1841

Lone I Walk at Night

Lone I walk at night upon the highway;
In a mist the stony road gleams far.
Still the night; to God the barren listens,
And each star speaks softly to each star.

In the skies what majesty and wonder!
Field and wood dream in a haze of blue.
Why unresting then my troubled spirit?
Do I wait on days of hope anew?

Nothing more I hope among the living,
Nothing of my past I now regret;
All I ask—the hour of peace and freedom;
All I wish—to sleep and to forget.

In my grave—O not in cold and darkness—
Would I lie in my eternal rest! . . .
Let me feel the pulse of life undying
Stir forever softly in my breast;

Let all night, all day, a voice enchanted
Sing of love to me above my grave,
And one oak with shadows wide, resounding,
Ever green above me watch and wave.

1841

The Princess of the Sea

The prince was swimming his horse in the sea.
He heard: "O my prince! Pray, look upon me!"

The horse started aside and snorted in dread,
In fear of the billows, while plunging ahead.

"I am a king's daughter," he heard at his side;
"Till morning with me in my chamber abide."

Then rose up in foam a hand whiter than milk
And reached for the bridle embroidered in silk.

Then up came a head surpassingly fair;
The seaweed was twined in plaited gold hair.

Her blue eyes were shining with love and desire;
The spray on her throat was a necklace afire.

Said the prince to himself: "I'll have you, my fair!"
And boldly the maiden he seized by the hair.

His hand was like steel; in her agony
She wept and struggled in vain to be free.

He swam to the shore in triumph and pride,
And called his companions to come to his side.

He called: "O comrades, come quickly to me
And look at the captive I've caught in the sea!

"Why stand you together and silently stare?
My captive is wondrous; my maiden is fair!"

The prince turned around, the youth overbold;
His triumph grew dull, and his merriment cold.

Before him he saw on the shimmering strand
A creature half-woman, half-snake, on the sand.

Her tail was dark-green, her bosom was white;
And, dying, her body trembled with fright.

The foam from her tresses fell soft as the rain,
And slowly her eyes grew darker with pain;

She wearily clutched the sands with a moan;
She murmured reproaches in accents unknown.

The prince rode away, and sadder was he.
The prince will remember the maid of the sea.

1841

Not For You My Love

No, not for you my love and inward glow,
And not for me your grace and beauty shining;
I love in you my grief of old and pining,
My fairest youth departed long ago.

And when at times I watch your eyes, I seem
To gaze with longing deep beyond the years.
I dream a wondrous voice within the spheres,
But not of you my heart's abiding dream.

I feel her kindred spirit as a flame,
And in your face her dearest face I see—
Her eyes that will no longer smile on me,
Her lips that never more will speak my name.

1841

The Prophet

Because the Judge of Life decreed
For me the gift of prophecy,
In eyes of humankind I read
Pages of sin and enmity.

I came declaring unto men
God's truth and love from age to age;
My kinsmen and my neighbors ran
And stoned me blindly in their rage.

I scattered ashes on my head,
And fled unto a desert place,
Where, like the birds of Heaven fed,
I live by God's unbounded grace.

All living creatures far and near
By God's command obey my voice;
The shining stars lean down to hear,
And when I speak the stars rejoice.

But when through noisy markets, bent,
I hasten on my lonely way,
With mocking smiles of self-content
The elders to the children say:

"Look, children, look! He was too proud
To live with us in peace and fame.
He called us to believe, and vowed
He rose to speak in God's own name.

"Behold him, mark his shame and dress!
How pale he looks, how poor and base!
Behold the fool in his nakedness,
How men despise him to his face!"

1841

NARRATIVE POEMS

The Lay of Kaláshnikov the Merchant

All hail to you, Tsar Iván Vasílevich!
About you we made our story and song,
About your favorite young bodyguard,
And of the fearless merchant Kaláshnikov.
Our song we made in the ancient way,
And sang to the tune of the dulcimer;
We recited and chanted the tale again.
Good Christian folk had joy in our song,
And boyar Matvéy Romodánovsky
Gave each a goblet with mead to the brim,
And his fairest lady presented with praise
Her own gift to us on a silver tray,
A towel embroidered with silken thread.
Three days and nights we sat at the feast;
They listened, they called for our song again.

I

It is not the sun in the shining sky,
Nor the clouds that rejoice in its light,
But the mighty Tsar Iván Vasílevich
In his crown of gold at the banquet hall.
Behind him stood all his serving-men,
The boyars and princes before his face,
And the bodyguards to the right and left.
The Tsar was feasting to the glory of God,
To his heart's delight and exceeding joy.

Then, smiling, the Tsar gave his command
To fill his own goblet of chased gold

With the sweet red wine from beyond the seas,
And to bear it around to his bodyguards.
They drank, and praised the name of the Tsar.

But one of the band of the bodyguards,
A sturdy youth and brave warrior,
Did not wet his lips in the golden cup.
He cast to the earth his eyes in gloom,
And upon his breast his head sank low;
In his mind his thought was a bitter thought.

The Tsar in his anger knit his eyebrows
And turned on the youth his piercing glance,
As gazes a hawk from the azure skies
On a turtle-dove of the grey-blue wings;
But the stalwart youth never raised his eyes.
Thereupon the Tsar brought down his staff
In his wrath, and its point of iron sank deep
In the boards of the hewn oak floor.
The youth never trembled nor moved in fear.
Then spoke the Tsar with threatening words
And the youth aroused himself from his dream.
"Ho, there, my servant Kiribéyevich!
What disloyal thoughts do you hide from us?
Do you burn with envy at our great glory?
Are you weary perhaps of your faithful service?
When the moon comes out, the stars rejoice
That the heaven's ways are bright at their feet,
But the star that hides its face in the clouds
Will fall extinguished straight to the earth.
It is unbefitting for you, Kiribéyevich,
To disdain your Tsar in his feast and joy,—

For you from your birth a Skurátov man,
Reared as a son in Malyúta's house!"

Then answered him the bodyguard,
Bowing lowly before the Tsar:

"O my lord and master, Iván Vasílevich!
Be not angry with me—unworthy slave:
My burning heart is not pleased with wine;
The feast will not ease my gloomy thoughts.
If I angered you, let your will be done
And my life cut short as punishment!
My head lies heavy, alas, on my shoulders,
And it sinks against my will to the grave."

To him then spoke Tsar Iván Vasílevich:
"What grief can trouble your gallant heart?
Is your brocaded mantle torn to shreds?
Is your cap of sable worn out with age?
Is your purse now empty of silver and gold?
Is your broadsword dull? your charger, lame?
Has a merchant lad knocked you down,
Defeated you in a boxing match?"

Then answered thus Kiribéyevich,
Tossing high his curly head:

"There lives no man who can vanquish me,
No man of merchant or of noble blood!
My charger is swift and sure in the race,
And my sword is keen, bright flashing as glass;
On holidays, by your favor, O Tsar,

I am clad as richly as other men.
When I mount my steed, my noble steed,
And ride up and down by the river,
With my sash of silk around my waist,
My rich velvet cap aslant on my head,
With its border of darkest sable fur,
At the carved gates of the houses I pass
Stand comely maidens and fair young wives,
And they gaze, admiring, whispering softly.
Only one does not look nor turn her head,
But she covers her face with her silken veil.

"In our motherland, in Holy Russia,
In vain you will seek for one as fair:
In every motion like a gliding swan,
In every glance like a tender dove,
In every word like a nightingale!
Like the rosy dawn in the morning sky
The bloom of roses upon her cheeks;
Her golden hair with bright ribbons bound
Falls in waving braids around her shoulders,
And caresses her bosom fair and white.
In a merchant house she was born and reared.
Alyóna Dmítrevna is the name she bears.

"When I look at her, my heart is troubled;
My arms, unnerved, grow weak in strength,
And my eyes grow dark as does the night.
I grieve and pine, O my gracious Tsar,
To remain in the world in loneliness!
I delight no more in my prancing steed,

I delight no longer in silk and brocade,
And I care no more for silver and gold!
With whom shall I share the gold I have?
To whom shall I show my daring strength?
Before whom shall I boast of my rich attire?

"Let me go alone to the Volga steppe,
Let me ride afar to the Cossack lands!
I will carry to death my restless head
And still my heart on an infidel's lance.
Let the savage Tartar warriors seize
My horse and sword, my trappings and gold.
Let the ravens drink the tears in my eyes,
Let my bones remain in the rain and sun;
Without burial rites let my dust be blown
On the plain to the ends of the world."

Then, laughing, said Tsar Iván Vasílevich:
"Well, my faithful servant, in your grief
And plight I will aid and comfort you.
Take my sapphire ring and string of pearls,
Seek out a matchmaker skilled and wise
And send by her hand these precious gifts
To your fair one—to Alyóna Dmítrevna.
If you win her love, make a wedding feast;
If you gain but scorn, do not fret at heart."

All glory to you, Tsar Iván Vasílevich!
But your wily slave has deceived your trust:
He did not speak the truth to you,
That the maid he loved was another's wife,

A young merchant's wife, in wedlock given
In the church of God by our Christian law.

🎵 🎵 🎵

   Sing cheer, my lads!
   Lift high a song of cheer!
   Drink free, my lads!
   Keep true your song with me!
For the fairest lady we'll sing our song again!
Sing joy to our lord and all his merry men!

II

The young merchant sat in the market-place,
The stalwart Stepán Paramónovich
Of the house and name of Kaláshnikov.
With care he spread out his silken wares,
Inviting the buyers with honeyed speech,
And counted his gold and silver coins.
A day without luck was this day for him:
The rich boyars passed by his booth
But did not enter to look at his wares.
The vesper bells had rung in the churches;
Beyond Kremlin walls the red sunset glowed;
The clouds in a mist overspread the sky,
Driven by a gathering whistling storm,
And soon was the market-place deserted.
Then the merchant Stepán Paramónovich
Made fast his booth with an oaken door
And a lock of cunning workmanship;
And close by the door, on an iron chain,
He left on watch his ferocious dog.

Then deep in thought he took his way
To his home and wife, across Moscow stream.
But when he entered his lofty house
Amazement seized Stepán Paramónovich:
No wife came out to the door to greet him;
Without cloth, the oaken table stood bare
And dimly flickered the icon lamp.
He called at once the old serving-woman.
"Come tell me, speak,Ereméyevna!
Where so late, at this hour of night,
Is my wife, Alyóna Dmítrevna?
And my little ones, are my children well?
I fear, worn out with games and playing,
They have fallen asleep in their little beds."

"O my master, Stepán Paramónovich!
This day, indeed, has been strange for me.
To the vespers she went, Alyóna Dmítrevna;
The priest and his wife returned long since.
They lighted their lamp, and sat down to dine,
And yet even now my mistress alone
Has not returned from the parish church.
And the children, worn out with play,
Are not asleep in their little beds,
But they cry for their mother with bitter tears."

Then a dreadful thought oppressed the heart
Of the brave young merchant Kaláshnikov.
He stood by the window, he gazed at the street;
The night gazed at him through the window.
The snow came down, flake upon flake,
Hiding the tracks of passing folk.

But sudden he heard a slamming door;
In the hall, the rush of a flying step;
He turned, he saw,—by the holy cross!
In the doorway stood his own young wife!
Pale she was, pale, and her head was bare,
As a wanton's her hair was dishevelled,
All covered with hoarfrost and snow;
Her eyes were staring as though not seeing,
And unmeaning words fell from her lips.

"O wife, my wife! where did you wander?
In what court, in what market-place?
Why untied your hair to all men's gaze,
And your dress disordered and torn?
You seem to come from a feast of love
With lewd young men, with boyars' sons!
Not for this, O wife, by the Virgin's shrine,
Have you and I our pledges made,
And in sign of love exchanged our rings!
I will lock you fast behind oaken doors
With iron locks, in a gloomy chamber!
You shall never see the light of day
And never again dishonor my name."

Hearing his words, Alyóna Dmítrevna
Grew deathly pale and trembled with fear,
Like an aspen leaf that shakes in the wind.
The bitter tears rolled down her cheeks;
She sank on her knees at her husband's feet.

"Alas, my lord, bright sun of my life!
Either hear me freely or bid me die!

Your words are sharper than many knives,
And they rend in two my troubled heart.
I fear not pain and a cruel death,
I fear not the slander of evil tongues,
But I fear too much your disfavor and hate.

"I was coming home from the parish church
Down the lone and desolate street,
When I thought I heard steps in the snow.
Then I saw a man run after me.
I felt my knees tremble with fear;
I covered my face with my silken veil.
But he caught my hands in his own hands,
And he spoke to me in a whisper low:
'Why fear you and tremble, my lovely one?
No thief am I and no highwayman,
But a bodyguard to the mighty Tsar,
For my name it is Kiribéyevich,
Of the house and fame of Malyúta!'

"My head spun round in darkness then,
And my fright was great on hearing his name;
He began to embrace and kiss me too,
And whispered thus, embracing me close:
'Answer, beloved, what things you desire,
My darling, light of my heart!
A necklace of pearls, brocade, or gold?
Or precious stones? Like a queen I'll dress you
To the envy and wonder of women you know;
But let me not die a mournful death,
Only love me, embrace me but once,

In farewell, before we must part!'
His caresses and kisses even now
Burn on my cheeks like a living flame—
His kisses accursed as the fires of Hell!
Through the gates the neighbors watched,
And they pointed their fingers at us.

"When I tore myself away from his arms
And ran headlong home, in the brigand's hands
I left in my flight my embroidered shawl,
Your gift at our wedding, and my silken veil.
He dishonored and shamed me forever,
A blameless woman, your honored wife. . . .
What evil of me will the spiteful speak!
And to whom shall I dare to show myself?

"Shield me, your wife, from the insults of men
And the mockery of all evil-doers!
In whom but you can I place my trust?
To whom but you shall I turn for help?
In the world I have long been an orphan;
My father has lain for years in his grave,
My mother beside him. My elder brother
Disappeared in a faraway land;
And my younger brother is only a child,
An innocent child, not wise in years."

Thus lamented Alyóna Dmítrevna,
Weeping her bitter, disconsolate tears.

Then sent Stepán Paramónovich
For his younger brothers to come in haste.
His two brothers came, they greeted him,

They lifted their voices and said to him:
"Now tell us true, our eldest brother,
What mischance has fallen upon your house
That you call us late in the dark of night,
On a windy night in the winter time?"
"I will tell you true, my brothers dear,
What sore mischance has befallen my house:
The Tsar's bodyguard, Kiribéyevich,
Has dishonored and shamed our honored name.
My soul will not bear this wrong in peace;
This evil my heart will never endure.
When tomorrow comes for the boxing match
In the Tsar's own sight on Moscow stream,
I will go to meet his bodyguard,
In a fight to the end, to my dying breath;
And if he should slay me, then you must fight
For the sacred truth, for our honored name.
Be not faint of heart, O brothers dear!
You are younger and greater in strength,
Your hearts are pure, your conscience clear,
And perchance the Lord will be merciful."

Then his brothers answered and said to him:
"Where blows the wind in the vaulted sky,
There the clouds hasten in obedience;
When the eagle calls with a mighty cry
On the plain of fight, on the plain of death,
To the feast of blood to devour the slain,
The young eagles do flock to his call.
You are the first in our father's place:

It is yours to say what is right and good,
And we go with you—one flesh and blood."

⚜ ⚜ ⚜

    Sing cheer, my lads!
    Lift high a song of cheer!
    Drink free, my lads!
    Keep true your song with me!
For the fairest lady we'll sing our song again!
Sing joy to our lord and all his merry men!

III

Over Moscow the great and golden-domed,
Over Kremlin's ancient walls and towers,
From beyond blue hills and forest lands,
Bright smiling on gabled roofs and porches,
The morning arose in glory of light,
Driving the clouds away from the sky.
She flung her golden hair in the azure
And bathed her face in crystal snow;
Like a beauty seeing herself in a mirror,
She beheld her face in the sky, and smiled.
Say, wherefore awake, O glorious dawn?
For what joy are you shining today?

They came, they gathered from every place,
Bold fighting men and challengers,
For the boxing match on the river's ice,
To amuse themselves on the holiday.

Then came the Tsar with his mighty train,
His boyars and all his bodyguards,
And he bade them stretch a silver chain,
A pure silver chain with links of gold.
They measured off a wide open place
Fifty paces long for the boxing bout.
Thereupon the Tsar bade his heralds call
In a ringing voice to the multitude:
"Come forth brave lads and fighting men!
Come forth and prove your strength and skill!
Come forward now to the silver ring!
Him who will win, the Tsar will reward;
Him who is beaten, the Lord will forgive!"

Then first came forth Kiribéyevich,
And he bowed in silence before the Tsar.
He threw from his shoulders his velvet coat;
His right hand he placed in pride on his hip,
With his left he smoothed his scarlet cap,
And waited to meet his challenger.
Three times the heralds shouted the summons,
But no champion for the fight came forth;
They stood and whispered, nudging each other.

Inside the ring the bodyguard strode,
And, mocking, he laughed at the timid fighters:
"Why so meek, my lads? Why like anxious men?
Take heart! I say for the holiday's sake
I will spare for penance your life and soul.
Only come to the fight to please our Tsar."

On a sudden the crowd parted its ranks
And forth came Stepán Paramónovich,

The young merchant, the brave champion,
Of the house and name of Kaláshnikov.
He bowed in reverence to the mighty Tsar,
To the Kremlin then and the holy churches,
And last he bowed to the Russian people.
His falcon eyes like two great flames
Stared fixedly at the bodyguard.
Then before his rival he took his place;
He drew on the gloves for the boxing bout;
He straightened back his powerful shoulders
And stroked with his hand his curly beard.

And thus Kiribéyevich spoke to him:
"I pray you, good youth, declare to me
Of what clan you are and what origin,
What name you bear among honest men.
I would know for whom to chant the Mass
And of whom to boast my victory."

Then answered him the brave merchantman:
"My name among men is Stepán Kaláshnikov,
And I was born of an honest sire;
In God's commands I've lived all my life.
I have never shamed my neighbor's wife,
Never lain in wait, a thief in the night,
Never hid my face from the light of day.
You have spoken well in words of truth.
For one of us they will chant the Mass,
And no later than tomorrow's noon;
Only one of us will rejoice and feast
With goodly comrades in pride of strength.

Not in jest or sport, for the crowd's delight,
I am come today, you infidel's son!
I am come to fight to the bitter death!"

When he heard these words, Kiribéyevich
Grew pale in his face like the winter snow;
His merry eyes grew dark and troubled,
And a chill ran through his mighty frame.
His words died away on his parted lips.

Then in silence the fighters drew apart.
On the ice in silence their combat began.

The bodyguard was the first to strike
A crashing blow on the merchant's breast.
He staggered, Stepán Paramónovich!
On his breast he wore a cross of copper
With a sacred relic from Kiev town,
And the cross was driven deep into his flesh,
And the blood as dew from beneath it flowed.
Then said in his heart Stepán Paramónovich:
"What is fated to be, it shall come to pass;
I will stand for truth to the very last."
He made steady then, he poised himself,
And with gathered strength he caught his foe
On the side of the head with a swinging blow.
The young bodyguard gave a feeble groan;
He swayed, he fell to the frozen ground,
On the frozen field, like a sapling pine,
Like a pine tree fallen in forest gloom
When the axe is laid at the roots.
When he saw this deed, Tsar Iván Vasílevich

In anger stamped his foot on the ground;
Great wrath as a cloud was black on his brows.
He bade his guards to seize the merchantman
And bring him at once before his face.

Thus spoke to him the orthodox Tsar:
"O answer me truly, answer in faith,
With intent and will or against your will
Have you slain my faithful bodyguard,
My best fighting man Kiribéyevich?"

"I will tell you true, most orthodox Tsar!
With intent and will I have slain my foe,
But wherefore and why I will not say;
I will tell this thing to my God alone.
O give your command to put me to death,
And I will proudly lose my guilty head.
But be merciful, I pray in my death,
To my little babes and my widowed wife,
And show your favor to my brothers twain."

"It is well for you, O goodly youth,
You merchant's son, brave fighting man,
You answered me on your conscience true.
To your widowed wife and orphaned babes
I will grant a gift from my treasury;
Your brothers twain from this day shall trade
Without tithe or tax in the Russian land;
But as for yourself, O fearless youth,
On the block lay down your restless head!
I will bid the axe to be sharp and keen,
I will robe my headsman for the holiday.

The great bell will toll your passing knell,
And all Moscow will remember and say
That you received my favor as well."

The church bells tolled in Moscow town,
Spreading afar the tidings of sorrow,
And throngs came soon to the market-place.
On lofty ground where the scaffold rose,
In his scarlet shirt with shining rubies,
Swinging his axe made keen and sharp,
And rubbing his naked hands in delight,
The headsman strode before the crowds.
He waited his victim, the merchantman.
And the merchant's son, the stalwart youth,
Embraced his brothers in a last embrace.

"O my brothers, my flesh and blood,
Let us kiss again, embrace one another,
Before I leave you forever in death.
Greet my wife Alyóna Dmítrevna,
And say to her not to grieve for me,
Not to speak of my death to my little ones.
Greet for me our ancient hearth,
Greet for me my comrades and kin,
And pray for me in the Church of God.
Pray for my soul—my sinful soul."

And thus he died, Stepán Paramónovich,
By a cruel death, by a death of shame,
And beneath the axe from the bloody block
On the scaffold fell his fair young head.

Beyond Moscow stream, they dug his grave
In the open field where three highways meet—
From Túla, Riazán, and Vladímir towns.
On his grave they heaped a mound of earth;
On the mound they set a maplewood cross.
The winds of the plain there howl and sing
O'er the lonely grave that bears no name.
The good folk pass by on their several ways:
Let an old man pass—he will cross himself;
Let a young man pass—he will gaze in pride;
Let a maiden pass—she will shed a tear;
Let a minstrel pass—he will make a song.

* * *

    Hey comrades bold and young!
    Hey minstrels of good song!
    Hey voices full and strong!
The beginning was true, let the end be true!
Come honor the name to whom honor is due!
        To our generous boyar glory!
        To his fairest lady glory!
        To all good Christians glory!

1837

The Fugitive
A Legend of the Caucasus

Haroun ran swifter than the deer,
Or hare before the eagle's flight,
When, mastered by his craven fear,
He quit his comrades in the fight.
His sire and brothers on the field,
For right and independence dying,
Their honor with their death had sealed,
Their noble blood for vengeance crying.
Haroun, to shame and duty dead,
Flung gun and sword in haste aside
Upon the battlefield, and fled.

The daylight waned; the rolling tide
Of evening mist on every hand
Shrouded the plain and mountainside;
The breeze from out the East blew cold,
And high above the Prophet's land
The peaceful moon was burnished gold.

All weary and athirst, his face
Begrimed by blood and reeking sweat,
Haroun beheld in moonlight, set
Among the crags, his native place.
He came by stealth; the village lane,
Deserted, lay in stillness bathed
When from the bloody field, unscathed,
Haroun came creeping home again.

He stopped before a cabin door
And entered, ready for the meeting
With news about the hapless war.
He hailed the elder with a greeting.
Selim scarce recognized his guest;
Selim lay ill with dark unrest
And knew that he was dying slowly.
"Allah is great! His angels holy
Preserve your fame, your life from harm."
"What news?" Selim with labored breath
Implored, his dimming eyes ablaze
With hope, his heart with war's alarm
Fast beating in the hour of death.
"We held the Pass for two long days.
My father fell; my brothers died.
A hunted beast, I crept to hide
Within the wilderness alone;
I dragged my bleeding feet in sand
Through fields of briar and of stone,
The tracks of wolves and boars my guide.
Circassia's crushed, our ancient land!—
Shelter me! By the Prophet, friend,
I'll be your slave unto my death!"
"Begone!" the dying cried in wrath,
"No shelter here for you, or bread!
My curse upon a coward's head!"
With secret shame before his own,
Haroun in silence left,—alone
Again outside old Selim's door.
He paused a moment once while passing
A new-made hut: A dream of yore
Rose in his memory, caressing

His throbbing temples with a kiss,
And soon his heart grew light with bliss.
He felt within the gloom of night
Soft glowing eyes of tender light,
And mused: She waits alone for me!
He stood, he listened yearningly,
He heard a song of old. . . . Haroun
Grew paler than the pallid moon:

> In the sky the moon
> Goes forth in light;
> A brave lad will soon
> Go forth to fight.
> For a lad unafraid,
> The song of a maid:
> My dearest, be brave
> And fear no alarm,
> Your prayer will save
> And keep you from harm.
> Be true to your name!
> Who fears to give
> His life unto fame,
> A coward will live:
> For a coward
> No stone or grave!
> For a coward
> The death of a slave!
> In the sky the moon
> Goes forth in light;
> A brave lad will soon
> Go forth to fight!

Haroun pursued in shame his way;
With lowered head and burning tears
He wept in anguish and dismay.
Then suddenly he saw gleam white
The cottage of his childhood years
Leaning against the storms of night,
And, comforted by hope again,
He knocked upon the window-pane.
He mused that in the hut another
Remained awake for him alone;
There deep in prayer his aged mother
Waited, he thought, to meet her own.
"Open, mother! I'm faint and worn!
It is I, Haroun, your youngest born,
Home unharmed from the Russian fire!"
"Alone?" "Alone." "And where your sire?
Your brothers?" "Slain. The Prophet give
Them peace, their souls in Paradise."
"Did you avenge them?" "As I live,
I hastened as the arrow flies;
I left my sword in a foreign land,
To come to you to dry your eyes."
"Silence, giaour! With sword in hand
You feared upon the field to die!
Away, and live with shame, apart,
O slave, deserter, in my heart
No son of mine!" A mother's cry,
Thus fell her stern denunciation,
And through the sleeping village long
Rang in the night their cries of wrong,
Sighs, curses, words of lamentation.
At last his dagger-stroke descended;

Haroun his life of shame had ended.
His mother saw him where he died,
At dawn, and coldly turned aside....
Haroun lay in his death unfriended,
Denied the hallowed burial ground.
Thus every straying village hound
Might lap his blood, and boys at play
Might pause to scorn him where he lay,
And long tradition might recall
A coward's shame, a coward's fall....
His homeless soul, in fear and doom,
Departed from the Prophet's eyes.
When light upon the mountain dies,
He wanders, homeless, in the gloom.
He knocks on a cottage door again,
He raps upon a window-pane;
But if he hears the Koran read
In faith, he flees in mist again
As once in craven fear he fled.

1838

The Novice

I did but taste a little honey ...
and, lo, I must die.
                            —I Samuel, 14:43

I

A cloister stood not long ago
Where Kúra and Arágva flow
Together in their seething race,
Like sisters locked in an embrace.
A pilgrim passing near the place
Today can see the crumbling shrine
Fallen in ruin and decline;
No censer swings in evening rays
A fragrant cloud; no hymn of praise,
No chant divine ascends these days.
One gray-haired monk of feeble breath,
Forgotten both by men and death,
Wanders among the tombs alone
Or brushes clean the mossy stone
Where letters, dimly seen, proclaim
A mountain chief of vanished fame,
Who, troubled and beset, laid down
Before the Tsar his tribal crown. . . .
Then peace and bounty unto men
Of Gruzia came: In every glen
And valley then she bloomed again,
Secure from foes and unafraid
Behind the steel of Russian aid.

In Russian, "The Novice" is known by the Georgian title, *Mtsyri*.

2

A Russian general rode down
The hills one day to Tiflis town.
He brought a captive, fallen ill
Along the mountain journey, still
A child six summers old or less,
A shy wild fawn in fearfulness,
Frail as a reed. The fever fires
The rugged spirit of his sires
Aroused in him; without a sigh
He put all food in silence by
As though in pride he wished to die.
A friendly monk in pity gave
Him care and saved him from the grave;
And thus, among the meek and true,
Behind monastery walls he grew.
He shunned the games all children play;
He fled from strangers in dismay.
He wandered silent and alone,
Gazed eastward to a land unknown,
And wasted from some secret ills
And dreams of home beyond the hills.
By steady discipline erelong
He came to speak the foreign tongue,
To be baptized, and vow before
The aged monks forevermore
To share in faithfulness their life,—
Beyond the world of gain and strife.
But suddenly one stormy night
He fled his cell. At early light
They sought him in the gloomy wood

And thickets where the cloister stood.
Three days they searched the wood in vain;
They found him, senseless, on a plain,
And bore him to his cell again.
They watched with grief his slender form
By hunger, suffering, and storm
Worn out. Each day he grew more weak,
But steadily refused to speak;
It seemed the end was all too near.
At last the aged friar dear
To him came pleading at his side.
The novice listened in his pride,
Then raised himself with all his strength
In bed, and thus he spoke at length:

3

"You come to hear me, father! Well,
My story I am glad to tell,
The burden of my heart to ease
At last, that I may die in peace.
I lived a slave, but never man
I harmed, and now my little span
Of life is over. Can I disclose
The inward truth my spirit knows?
I've lived so little, all my life
A captive. For an hour of strife
In nature, oh, two lives I would
Surrender gladly if I could!
One dream to me in prison came;
One passion burning like a flame
I knew in my captivity.

A gnawing worm, it lived in me;
It roused my thoughts of liberty;
It called me from my cell and prayer
To freedom, life,—to live and dare
Among the cliffs that pierce the sky,
Where men, like eagles, live on high.
This flame of passion in the night
I fed with tears I wept. In sight
Of God and man I own this day
My pride, and no forgiveness pray.

4

"Father, I've heard it said for long
You saved my life when I was young.
But why? A child morose and lone,
A driven leaf by tempests blown,
I lived in gloom, behind a gate—
A child in soul, a monk by fate.
Within your walls I never heard
That holiest and sweetest word
Of *mother* that all children know;
You hoped that I would soon outgrow
Its spell and memory. In vain:
The undying word as a refrain
I loved from birth. Others I knew
Had parents, friends, and kindred true
At home; but I, of my own kind,
No dead or living soul could find.
Then unavailing tears no more
I wept, and in my heart I swore
A vow that some day, for an hour,

With all compassion in my power,
I would embrace a kindred near,
In all the world to me most dear.
Alas! my dream and burning vow
Are dead in all their splendor now;
And, as I lived, I die—a slave
And orphan in an alien grave.

5

"I do not fear the grave, for there
Will sleep my suffering and care
In dreamless, cold eternal peace.
I'd like to live, and never cease
To dream! I'm young, O father, young!
Have you forgotten then how strong
The dream of freedom in a boy
Endures?—How pure a thing is joy!
How deep the secret wonder when
We watch the sun go down on glen
And field, or when on a mountain peak,
Where winds are sweeping chill and bleak,
We spy within a cleft of stone
A creature from a land unknown—
A pigeon cowering close and warm
In terror at the thunderstorm!
You would renounce and thrust away
This bit of beauty! But you are grey
And frail from age; you crave no more!
You have something to forget before
You die—and something yet to give.
You have lived! Oh, I too would live!

6

"You wish to know what I have seen
In freedom?—Meadows waving green
In sunlight rays, and mountains crowned
With woods luxuriant around,
Resounding in their green advance
Like brothers in a circling dance.
I saw the massive cliffs cut through
By swollen torrents, and I knew
The doom that brooded in their heart,
For heaven gave to me the art
Of deeper sight. The cliffs, apart,
Reached far across dividing space,
Their stone arms yearning to embrace
Again; but days and ages fleet
Will pass, and ne'er the cliffs shall meet.
I saw the crests of mountains white
Loom strange and wonderful in light
At break of day when summits high,
Like smoking altars in the sky,
Arise within the azure blue.
I saw the clouds in crowds anew
Come slowly from their beds of mist
To wander toward the sacred East,
As might a caravan of birds arise
To sail in light across the skies.
Above the mists, in robes of snow,
Like diamonds in the sky aglow,
I saw the Caucasus. I know
Not why my heart felt sudden light,
Or what the cause of my delight.

Some inner voice said secretly
That once those peaks had nurtured me,
And in my memory at last
Rose clear, and clearer yet my past.

7

"Plainly I saw a deep ravine
As in a dream, our home between
The trees, and in the mountain pass
The village huts. In tallest grass
I heard the drove of horses neigh
At evening on their homeward way,
And dogs in twilight bay. And then
I saw a group of sunburnt men
Who came, experienced in war,
To sit before my father's door.
I saw their scabbards in a beam
Of moonlight shine, and in a dream
There clear within my memory
The scenes of childhood came to me:
My father stood in battle dress,
Alive in stately fearlessness
Before me. And I saw again
His flashing sword and glinting chain,
His glances resolute with pride.
I heard my sisters at my side
Who sang with unconstrained delight;
I saw their eyes of tender light
Above my cradle in the night. . . .
I heard the brook sing on its way
In our ravine, where I came to play

Along a golden sandy bay.
I watched the swallows veering low
As when they skimmed above the flow
Or swiftly soared in air again
Before the coming of the rain.
At last I knew my home on earth,—
The tales remembered since my birth
About our tribal games and frays,
The tales of vanished ancient ways
Of life, and happier better days.

8

"And what my life, while I was free?
I lived—in blissful joy for three
Full days! My earthly pilgrimage
Could be as sad as your old age,
And gloomier, had I never known
This rapture now I call my own!
Long, long ago I vowed I'd go
To see how fair the earth, to know
If man as freeman or as slave
Must live from birth unto his grave.
Then in the night, a night of dread,
When, fearful and uncomforted,
You lay in prayer upon the floor
Beside the altar, I fled before
The thunderstorm. Out, out in space,
The wind and thunder to embrace,
I fled. I hailed the clouds and lands!
I caught the lightning in my hands! . . .
What gift of life is yours to give
Within this prison where you live,

To gratify that friendship warm
Between my wild heart and the storm?

9

"And so I ran, but where, how far,
I hardly knew. No kindly star
Came out to light my troubled way.
But I was strangely glad and gay
To breathe the freshness of the wood
And rain. Yes, that alone was good!
I ran for hours until I sank
Exhausted on a grassy bank,
To listen in my hiding place
With trembling for the sound of chase.
The storm grew slowly still. On high,
Between the earth and darkling sky,
I saw a strip of pallid light,
And faint against it in the night
The jagged peaks. Deep in the grass
I lay in silence. Far down the pass
I heard a jackal's human cry;
I saw a serpent gliding by
Among the rocks. I did not fear.
I felt myself in kinship near
The beasts, and like a beast I ran
Or hid myself—in fear of man.

10

"A swollen flood in a deep ravine
Below me thundered far, unseen,
Resounding in a wild loud tongue

As if a thousand voices strong
In anger rose. I understood
The ever-roaring multitude,
The speech of waters striving long
In silence or in storm, but strong
In never-ending war, alone
Against the stubborn crags of stone.
Then sudden in the greying mist
The birds began to sing; the East
Turned rose and gold; in leaf and wood
The breezes waked in solitude;
The flowers breathed. From where I lay,
I too arose to greet the day....
I looked about; I will not say
I had no fear: I saw I lay
Beside a swirling waterfall
Below a cliff of rocky wall,
Where walked at night a demon lone
Along the steeps of giant stone,
When, from the gates of heaven hurled,
He sank within the nether world.

II

"The earth was like a garden wide
With bloom, adorned in light, in pride
Of rainbow hues and tears divine.
The twining tendrils of the vine
In bright translucent leaves of green
Made graceful draperies between
The trees, where grapes in clusters hung
Like precious earrings, and among

Them fluttered, timorous and shy,
Each wondrous bird and butterfly.
I sank upon the grass again
And listened to the magic strain
And whisperings that ran between
The bushes circling the ravine,—
Their talk of mysteries that rise
Upon the earth and in the skies.
In one exulting voice the tide
Of wood and field on every side
Made one great chorus; man alone
No praise uplifted to the throne
Of life. And oh the joy sublime
And grace that filled me at that time!
That dream I would today regain
If but to live the dream again.
The sky that morning was so near
To me, so pure, the air so clear,
My wakeful mind could see in light
Of azure deep the angels' flight.
I never saw so deep, so blue
A sky; eye, heart, and mind it drew,
And after them my spirit flew.
I lay within a dream immersed
Till roused by noonday heat and thirst.

12

"Then downward toward the cooling tide
I started, clutching at the side
Of yielding shrub and naked steep.
And oft a stone dislodged would sweep

The mountain, crashing with a bound,
And sink below with splashing sound,
Leaving upon a gust of wind
A trailing cloud of dust behind.
I strove and toiled with heaving breath
For youth is unafraid of death.
At last I reached the level way.
There in the coolness of the spray
I joyed, and, kneeling at the brink,
I greedily began to drink.
And then I heard a voice! In haste
I fled, and hid within the waste
Of bushes, trembling in my dread;
But soon, composed, I raised my head
And listened eagerly again.
The voice came nearer, nearer. Then
I knew it was a Gruzian maid.
So artless, gay, and unafraid
She sang, it seemed that love alone
And friendship sweet in ways unknown
Inspired her open-hearted lay.
I hear her simple song today
At twilight when her spirit sings
Unseen to me, and comfort brings.

13

"She bore a pitcher on her head,
Descending to the river bed
Along a narrow path of stone;
And, tripping, to herself alone
She mocked her own unsteadiness

With girlish glee. Her tribal dress
Was plain and poor. Light-spirited,
With streaming veils behind her head,
She moved. Her face the summer sun
Had tinted golden for his own;
Her parted lips suffused with fire,
Her eyes with light of sweet desire
So deep, so warm her wondrous eyes
With mysteries of maiden sighs,
I grew confused. Within my heart
The wonder and the sudden smart
I still recall as in a dream—
Her pitcher gurgling in the stream,
The rustling sounds, and nothing more.
When I looked up, I saw she bore
The pitcher balanced on her head
As home she turned with quiet tread;
As graceful as a poplar tree,
She moved on lightly, cautiously.
I saw beside a boulder bare
Two hovels like a friendly pair,
Their smoke blue-curling in the air;
Then slowly, silently, a door
Was opened wide and shut once more.
I know you will never understand
My heart of grief. I'm glad, my friend,
You do not know my misery!
So let my secret memory
Alone live on, and die with me.

14

"Fatigued, I lay in weariness
Within the shade. With tenderness
A slumber closed my eyes, but plain
In my troubled dream I saw again
The coming of the Gruzian maid.
A host of strange sweet yearnings swayed
With anguish deep my aching breast,
And from my sighing and unrest
Of night I woke. The pale moon shone
Above me dimly, and alone
Behind her stole a little cloud,
As if to clasp her captive proud
And swallow greedily her prey.
The world in gloom and silence lay.
Afar the snowy peaks shone clear
With hems of silver lace, and near,
In silence, fainter than before,
The river splashed upon the shore.
In the familiar hut a light
First died, then flickered in the night:
Thus in the midnight sky a star
With trembling burns and dies afar!
I yearned for her but did not dare
To go. One aim was mine, one care—
To find my home! I overcame
My hunger and my heart aflame,
And then, in fear, I took my flight
In tangled woods and dark of night.
The mountains vanished from my sight;
And soon in forest gloom astray
I knew I'd lost in the night my way.

15

"In vain with bursts of mad despair,
I tore the brake and bush with bare
Despairing hands. The woods lay wide.
The giant woods on every side
In drearier walls began to loom
Each hour. Deep night alone, in gloom,
In leaf and branch with sullen sighs
Stared at me with a thousand eyes.
With reeling brain, in darkness blind,
I climbed the trees. I climbed to find
My way again. The woods rose high
Far to the edges of the sky.
I fell upon the ground in wild
Distraction, sobbing as a child
In my infirmity; I rent
The earth, in my bewilderment,
And burning tears without a sound
Ran endlessly into the ground. . . .
Believe me, helpless, even then
I felt estranged and far from men;
And had a cry for help been wrung
From me, I swear I would have flung
Away my weak and craven tongue.

16

"You know that in my childhood years
I never shed, in weakness, tears;
But lying there I felt no shame
For tears I wept within the frame
Of night, beneath the trees and **moon**!

And then in moonlight rays I soon
Beheld a little open ground
Of moss and sand hemmed all around
By forest walls. A shadow flew
Across the grass, two sparks of blue
Swift flame, as with a sudden bound
A beast leaped to the open ground,
And rolled, or lay supine in sand.
The panther of the desert land
I saw before me. Long he clawed
His prey; with whining loud he gnawed
A bone, then turned his bloody gaze
To the full moon, his hair ablaze
Like silver in the streaming light.
I seized a bough, and in the night
I stood; I waited for the fight,
My heart within me flaming hot,
Athirst for blood. . . . Ah yes! my lot
Seems like a strange, unhappy fate;
But now I know, although too late,
I might have had a manful place
Among the bravest of my race.

17

"I waited. In the dark of night
He scented danger; in moonlight
He growled, and, mournful like a sigh,
His growl rose through the woods. Then high
He reared, he fiercely tore the ground,
And, crouching lower, at a bound
He sprang at me with savage wrath.

But I was quick in the face of death.
My blow descended swift and true;
I clove his blunt wide forehead through
As with an axe, and drove again.
He groaned, as groans a man in pain;
He fell, but in a moment more,
Although his blood began to pour,
He sprang up, fighting for his life.
Our battle boiled, our mortal strife!

18

"He threw himself upon my breast.
Between his jaws I thrust and pressed
My club; I twisted it twice round
Inside his throat; upon the ground
Together, like two snakes enlaced
And closer than two friends embraced,
We rolled, and in the gloomy night
We waged in wrath a deadly fight.
I was in a frenzy then; I had
Become a beast, with snarling mad;
I raged, I bellowed even as he,
As though by nature born to be
A wolf or panther of the wood
And comrade of the forest brood.
It seemed I had forgotten long
The cadence of our human tongue,
As if from childhood I had known
No accent save the savage groan,
The fearful howl and cry alone.
At last my foe gave in, his breath
Came faint, and, writhing as in death,

He clutched me in a last embrace.
His eyes within his rigid face
Grew stern a moment, staring deep,
Then closed in soft eternal sleep.
Thus face to face, with warlike pride,
As men in war, unterrified,
He met his foe, and bravely died.

19

"But, look! The cuts upon my breast
And scars from baneful claws attest
They have not closed, they have not healed!
But soon within the grave concealed
The earth will bind them up afresh,
And death shall heal my broken flesh. . . .
I did not wait; my little strength
I gathered, groaning, and at length
I wandered in the woods again. . . .
I struggled with my fate in vain:
Fate mocked me in my bitter pain.

20

"When from the woods I came, the day
Awoke; the infinite array
Of stars then faded in the light,
And misty woods resounded bright
With morning song. Afar, the smoke
From huts arose, and voices woke
With morning winds across the glen.
I listened—how familiar then
The scene appeared! I gazed on day,

I gazed in terror either way! . . .
I saw my prison world again;
I knew my fleeing was in vain.
I found it hard to comprehend
At first my hopes at last must end,
After all my woes of many days
And all my dreams on barren ways,—
For what? To learn I was from birth
Denied by fate God's perfect earth?
To feel the bliss of being free
With sounds of life in every tree,
Only to take into my grave
Vain dreams of home? to die a slave,
With hopes deceived, and bear the shame
At last of pity and of blame?
I thought it was a frightful dream,
My spirit dying in a gleam,
When suddenly the cloister bell
Rang through the valley, and its knell
Aroused me. Oh, I knew it well!
How oft it had destroyed my dear
Familiar dreams of home all near
To me, my dreams of open plains,
Of swift wild horses and campaigns,
Of wars among the cliffs on high
And victories beneath the sky!
I listened, weary, to the note
Of cloister bells; their ringing smote
My heart like iron. And I divined
In my despair I shall never find
My native home among my kind.

21

"But I have well deserved my fate.
A horse will shrewdly use his gait
To bring a clumsy rider prone,
And find, by instinct, to his own
The shortest way, without a rein.
But I, not so! I lay inane
And helpless with my vain desire.
I seemed a weak slow-dying fire,
A dream, a sickness of the brain
Infirm, the seat of evil bane
And prisoned youth. Thus grows a flower
Immured, alone, and paler hour
By hour, in dampness pent about,
Too frail to put its young leaves out,
But waiting for the living rays
To quicken it to brightness; days
Pass by till some compassionate
Fair hand, in pity at its fate,
Removes it to a garden where
With neighbor roses it may share
The sun and air. On every side
Life blooms in sweetness and in pride.
But lo! beneath the blazing skies
The poor spent flower droops and dies.

22

"Thus, like a flower, I thirsting lay
Beneath the flaming sun of day.
In vain I laid my weary head
Deep in the grass around me spread:

The withered leaves entwined in brown
My forehead with their thorny crown;
The earth itself in my retreat
Was breathing in my face with heat,
And sparks above me circled, fleet
And glittering, as a vapor white,
Along a glinting barren height
In spaces far. Earth, sky, and air
Lay silent, palsied with despair,
In fainting torpor, hollow-eyed.
If but a corncrake would have cried,
A cricket shrilled one cheery note,
Or but a mountain brook remote
Resounded near! . . . Only a snake,
The dry grass rustling in its wake,
Lay gleaming on its yellow back,
A sword resembling, marked from neck
To tail with golden spots and bands;
There, cautious in the shifting sands,
It glided, coiled in a triple ring,
An instant in the sun to spring,
And vanished quickly out of sight.

23

"The vault of sky hung blue in light
Above my head. Two mountains loomed
Afar in purple mist entombed,
And on the near one, rising tall,
I saw the cloister's jagged wall.
Arágva and Kúra ran below
Like silver fringes in their flow

Around the curving shores of green
And roots of underbrush between.
I tried to raise myself—the world
Around me reeled and madly whirled;
I tried to call—my tongue was dry
And soundless. In my fever I
Believed I heard my dying sigh
Where I lay thirsting.
                          In my dream
I thought I lay within a stream
Mysterious and deep as night,
That waters cold and pure as light
Flowed sweet into my breast—so sweet
I was afraid I might fall asleep.
Above my head in shelves of blue
The waves together ran while through
Their crystal clearness came a light
Far gentler than the moon at night.
There little fish of motley hue
Played glistening before my view,
Of which but one, more free than all
And far more friendly, I recall.
The scales upon her back were gold;
And, swimming closer, then more bold
Round and again above my head,
She glanced at me with furtive, sad
Green eyes so tender and so deep,
I gazed in wonder in my sleep.
And then I heard her silver strain
Sing soft a whispering refrain
To me, and cease, and sing again.

She sang to me: 'O stay, my child,
    In coolness here below!
O stay and be at peace, my child,
    Within the river's flow.

'Your weariness will pass, your fear
    And troubled glance,
For I will call my sisters here
    In a circling dance.

'Sleep softly in your bed of spray;
    Your coverlet is bright.
The years will come and pass away
    In golden dreams of light.

'My child, I give my love to you;
    I give you all my heart!
Like waves forever free and true,
    We shall never part!'

And long I listened in my dream.
It seemed to me the crystal stream
Within its peaceful murmur rang
Of words the little goldfish sang.
Then all the world went dark, the light
Died in my eyes, and, in my plight
And weakness, all my strength gave way.

24

"Thus I was found and borne away.
The rest you know. But I have done;

My story's ended. All is one
To me if you my tale believe
Or disbelieve. I only grieve
To think my body will not lie
At rest beneath my native sky
At home, that no one will proclaim
In truth my dark unhappy name,
And that my woes of how I strove
Shall never move a heart of love.

25

"Father, farewell! Give me your hand;
My own's on fire. Pray, understand
My burning faith from childhood days,
My soul with secret hope ablaze!
At last, unsatisfied, the flame
Bursts through the prison of my frame
And shall return to Him who knows
The reason for our earthly woes,
Who in the course of time bestows
Eternal peace. I little care
In what celestial holy air
My soul may find its paradise.
Alas! I would the bliss of skies
Give up for one brief hour at home
Among the cliffs I used to roam.

26

"I feel the seal of death today.
Before you go, I humbly pray
Bury my body in the place

Inside our garden, in the space
Between the white acacias; there
So golden is the summer air
In fragrant leaf and grasses deep,
I would forever lie in sleep,
Alone in death, and never sigh
Again for life and air and sky.
There looms the Caucasus in sight!
Perhaps its peaks of gleaming light
In cooling breeze and storm will blow
A farewell word to me below.
Perhaps a brother's whisper near
My grave in silence I shall hear,
And I will dream a spirit rare
Arises that with tender care
Wipes lovingly from off my brow
The sweat of death that gathers now,
And sings of home a farewell lay. . . .
I am at peace, and turn away
From hatred on my dying day."

1839

The Demon
An Eastern Tale

PART ONE

1

The exiled Demon winged his way
Above the earth of sin and crime,
And memories of days sublime
Rose in his mind in bright array
When in the realms of light and day
He shone amidst God's seraphim;
When comets in their courses fleeting
Were happy to exchange a greeting
And smile with tenderness on him;
When still he thirsted to achieve
Eternal knowledge and to trace
The caravans of stars in space;
When still he loved and could believe,
The happy first-born of Creation!
His mind untroubled by negation,
By fear or hate, or by the pain
Of barren, dreary centuries. . . .
But now these ancient memories
Of life were wearisome and vain.

2

He'd wandered long in banishment,
One homeless, one without an aim,
While ages after ages went
Like minutes endlessly the same,
Like endless eddies on a stream.

The earth was his: with rule supreme
He scattered joylessly the seeds
Of evil midst mankind, nor met
Resistance to the snares he set.
At last he wearied of his deeds.

3

The exiled Demon in his flight
Beheld the Caucasus below:
Kazbék with peaks of diamond light
Aglow in their eternal snow
And, lower, like a trail of night,
Like a writhing serpent darkly coiling,
The chasm Daryál; there Térek, boiling,
In fury like a lion roaring
Leaps thundering with bristling mane.
There beasts of prey and eagles soaring
Aloft within their azure plain,
Heed his reverberating roar.
There argosies of golden clouds
From southern lands in ranging crowds
Attend him to the Caspian shore.
There sullen cliffs in thronging masses
Enfolding a mysterious dream
Watch frowningly above the stream
The gleaming waters in the passes.
There, menacing among the mists,
Upon a cliff, a granite tower,
Like a giant watcher stern with power,
Stands guard against antagonists. . . .
All wild and wondrous lay about

The world God made. In desolation
He gazed with a disdainful glance,
And the universe of God's creation
He hated; weariness and doubt
Remained within his countenance.

4

Before him then another scene
Spread far of beauty fair and tender:
The Gruzian vales lay robed in green
Like carpets rich in woven splendor.
O fair, O blessed spot on earth
Where glancing rills with rippling mirth
O'er pebbled floors and stones that glisten
Run swiftly on; where nightingales
Sing to the rose nor pause to listen
For mates to answer to their tales;
Where sycamores with shade are wide;
Where deer in caverns come to hide
When drowsy with the burning tide,
While in the hum of myriad voices
And sweetly breathing leaf and flower
The land of song and light rejoices.
O sultry skies, the languid hour,
The aromatic dew of night,
And stars in their bewitching light
That shine in Gruzian eyes of love!
But naught of life and nature's splendor
Had power the Demon's heart to move
With strength or joy or feeling tender,
For all he looked upon he hated
Or else with scorn he contemplated.

5

A castle with a great wide yard
Goudál had long ago erected.
There slaves submissive and dejected
Through years of grief had labored hard.
From early dawn beyond the yard
Long shadows of its walls were thrown
On mountain slopes; rough hewn in stone
Below the rampart ran a flight
Of steps to swift Arágva's waters;
Here oft in veils of snowy white
Tamára, comeliest of his daughters,
Came tripping to the stream in light.

6

Long had the gloomy castle frowned
In silence grim on vales below.
Today, red wines in goblets flow
And gay with song the flutes resound.
Goudál his daughter's hand has plighted
And to his court his kin invited
To feast beside the gleaming fountains.
Among her girlhood friends the bride
Reclines; in song the moments glide
Too soon away. Behind the mountains
The sun goes down at eventide.
While clapping hands in rhythmic measure
They gaily sing, her tambourine,
Tamára, in their round of pleasure,
Starts ringing joyfully between
Her hands. She pauses, smiles, then flies

Aside; light as a bird she flashes
By while beneath her silken lashes
Shine radiant her glowing eyes.
She bows, her form with motion fleet,
Her raven eyebrows arching slightly
The while her graceful little feet
Are gliding on the carpet lightly;
And like a child in her bridal dress
Tamára smiles in her happiness.
A moonbeam for a moment dancing
Along a wave could not in truth
Transcend her joyful smile entrancing,
Her smile of innocence and youth.

7

I swear it by the midnight star,
By rays of light from East to West,
No mighty conqueror or tsar
On earth, no khan or shah afar
A fairer maiden has caressed!
I swear that in the burning hours
No wave of harem fountain splashing
Has quivered in the joy of dashing
On one so fair its pearly showers!
No mortal hand, I truly vow,
Has ever touched a fairer brow!
And since this world was first begun,
Since paradise was lost at birth,
No diviner shape upon this earth
Has bloomed beneath the southern sun!

8

For one last time she danced, elated.
Alas! another life awaited
Goudál's young heir, in wedlock fated,
Fair freedom's child, to live a slave
Immured within strange halls unknown
To her, with kinsmen not her own,
For good or ill unto her grave.
At times a hidden sense of doubt
Darkened Tamára's radiant face;
Yet was her artless charm throughout
So pleasing on that vigil night
In its true simplicity and grace,
That, had the Demon in his flight
Beheld her joy, he might have sighed
For lost angelic hosts of light,
And might have pitied the young bride.

9

The Demon saw.... A strange elation
And pangs of wondrous adoration,
With music of some blissful rest
And harmonies of spheres above,
Then filled his lonely barren breast
With beauty, holiness, and love.
He watched the scene before him, feeling
His dreams of old and his unrest,
The dreams arising in his mind
Like star upon a star, revealing
The bliss of Heaven left behind.
And fettered by an unseen power,

He felt a sadness strangely new,
And purer feelings came to flower
Again in ways of old he knew. . . .
Did these portend regeneration,
Denial of evil and temptation?—
God would not grant him to forget
The past, nor could the Demon yet
Himself forget and crave salvation.

10

Meantime, unsparing of his beast,
The bridegroom to the wedding feast,
Impatient, hastened on his way
Till safe he reached at close of day
Arágva's banks. Behind him, swinging,
The camels came in twilight glow
With tinkling bells, all stepping slow,
Their costly loads of presents bringing,
While Sanodhal's impatient lord
Guided the caravan along.
A leathern belt enclasped his strong
And supple form; his jeweled sword
And dagger flashed beneath the sun
And, at his back, his fine-chased gun.
His mantle fluttered in the breeze,
Its armlets gay with silken thread
And braids of gold embroideries;
His bridle shone; his spirited
Unrivalled steed of Caucas strain,
Of perfect shape and golden mane,
Came champing at his bit with dread,

With snorts, as from the cliff askance
He watched the foaming waters dance.
Here narrow and perilous the way
With crags to left, the flood to right,
Along the fearsome gorges lay.
The hour grew late. On the snowy height
The sunrays died; mists rose apace;
The horsemen quickened then their pace.

II

There stood a chapel by the road,
Since days of old the last abode
Of a chieftain sainted in the land
But slain by a revengeful hand.
Each pilgrim faring on his way
To feast with friends or join the battle
With ardent words would come to pray
At this forsaken mountain chapel,
Believing that his faith and prayer
Would save him from a Moslem slayer.
But bold the daring bridegroom sped,
Disdainful of the sacred dead:
The Demon turned his thoughts aside
With wily images of bliss
When in the night he dreamed his bride
Had yielded to his ardent kiss.—
Before him sudden rose two men,
And more! . . . A shot! Another! Then
Upon his ringing stirrups rising,
His cap pulled down, a raid surmising,
The gallant-hearted prince spoke not

A word; his long whip fiercely crashing,
Like an eagle from its eyrie dashing,
He charged the foe. Again a shot!
A cry of pain and stifled woe
Rang through the stillness of the valley.
Not long he fought the hidden foe;
His craven bands refused to rally.

12

Huddled together in the dead
Of night, the camels gazed in dread
Upon the fallen horsemen dying,
While in the dark untenanted
The silver bells resounded, sighing.
Plundered the precious caravan!
And soon the birds of prey began
To wheel above the dead at night.
Not theirs the Christian grave and rite
Nor sleep beneath the chapel stones
Where lie at rest their fathers' bones.
No sister and no mother weeping
Will come in sorrow, veiled, unsleeping,
To mourn a son's or brother's loss!
And yet upon this mountain way
Devoted hands will raise one day
Beneath the cliff a hallowed cross;
The ivy, in the springtime growing,
Will twine it with a fond caress,
With emerald nets of tenderness,
And there the weary, homeward going
Along the toilsome road and glade,
Will rest beneath the sacred shade.

13

The steed runs swifter than the roe,
And snorts as if to meet the foe.
Now wildly dashing in his flight,
Or listening to the winds of night,
He sniffs the air with nostrils wide,
He paws the rocky mountainside.
Then tossing his dishevelled mane,
His clanging iron hoofs resounding
In deepest darkness, onward bounding
He rushes fearlessly again.
A dying rider on his back!
His head lies on the horse's mane;
The reins, no longer held, fall slack.
His feet the stirrups press no more;
The flowing drops of blood run o'er
His face and saddle. Through the fight,
How brave the charger in his flight,
Like an arrow from the battle scene!
Alas! the shot of the Ossetien
Overtook his master in the night.

14

Goudál's great house was loud with weeping
And neighbors crowded in the court:
Whose horse in clouds of dust came leaping
And fell on flagstones at the fort?
And who the rider, cold and mute,
His frowning brow still resolute
With war's alarm and strife and pain?
One hand in maddening distress

Lay stiffened in the horse's mane;
With blood was stained his martial dress.
Too soon your wedding day was over,
O fairest bride!—The prince at least
Had kept his promise, and your lover
Came riding to the marriage feast.—
Alas! he would no more bestride
His swift and noble steed in pride.

15

Like a thunderclap, disaster dread
Fell on the happy house and swept
Their joy away; upon her bed
Tamára in her sorrow wept.
With grief her heavy heart was throbbing,
And burning tears betrayed her fear,
When, lo! between her grief and sobbing
It seemed a wondrous voice came near.

"Weep not, my child, you weep in vain!
Your tears will not awake again
His life with dew of living sighs.
They only burn your face with pain
And dim the light within your eyes.
His soul is far, and all your grieving
He cannot feel nor know your plight.
His unfettered soul is now receiving
The vision of celestial light
And hears the holy angels singing.
How vain all dreams of life and sighs
And maiden tears in sorrow springing

To him who dwells in Paradise!
Ah, no! no life in all creation,
No human fate, believe, is worth
Your suffering and tribulation,
O dearest angel of the earth!

>"O'er the boundless aery ocean,
>Star on star, like phantom sails,
>Soft with music of their motion
>Float within their misted veils.
>In the azure fields unending,
>Fleecy clouds that leave no trace
>In the skies their way are wending
>Through immeasurable space.
>Hour of parting, hour of greeting,
>Brings no joy to them or pain,—
>No regret when day is fleeting,
>Nor the hope for day again.
>In your hour of care and sorrow,
>Like the clouds afar in air,
>O remain upon each morrow
>As unmoved as they by care.

"When night shall draw her velvet veil
Upon the mountain peaks in shade,
And worlds as in a fairy tale
Enchanted into silence fade;
When every breeze of night that passes
Stirs on the cliff the withered grasses,
While in her hidden nest the lark
With gladness flutters in the dark;

When under branching vines the flower
Of night drinks eagerly the shower
Of scented dew; when in a swoon
In clouds shall come the silver moon,
And softly over the mountains rise
To gaze at you with furtive eyes,—
Then I will wing to you below,
Nor leave you till the Orient flashes,
And o'er your darkened silken lashes
My golden dreams will gently blow."

16

The words grew fainter in the air
And faded softly sound on sound.
Tamára, rising, looked around
With fear and rapture, but despair
Awakened in her breast at war,
And all transformed her feelings were
Within; a flame ran through her veins;
Her spirit burst its living chains,
While still a magic voice and daring
She heard like a refrain ensnaring.
Then gentle sleep, ere morning rose,
Over her weary eyes came stealing;
And yet a strange prophetic feeling
Disquieted the night's repose.
A silent form of love and grace
In light of wondrous beauty shining,
He came, above her couch inclining;
So tender, stern, his yearning face,
So infinite with grief and passion,

He seemed in truth to feel compassion.
But no angel of celestial birth,
And not her guardian on earth,
Not in a crown of rainbow rays
With glory in his hair and gaze;
Not Hell's accursed spirit, no!
No sinner, rebel, in his might!
He seemed a shape of twilight glow—
Not day or night, not gloom or light!

Part Two

I

"O father, father! do not blame me,
Be merciful and kind to me!
Behold my tears, O do not shame me,
My burning tears of misery!
In vain the suitors come a-wooing
To win my love, to have my life;
I'll never now to my undoing
Become another's bride and wife.
O do not chide me, father, pray!
I die for sorrow. Day by day
I'm troubled by an evil doom,
By a fiendish spirit torn in gloom
As in a dream unceasingly.
I perish! O pity, pity me!
For my unreason, father, send me
To a nun's abode for all my years,
And there my Saviour will defend me
And wash away my grief and tears.

No happiness has life to give me
In my bereavement! Let the gloom
And stillness of the cell receive me,
Let a convent be my living tomb."

2

And thus a convent far and lonely
Sheltered the hapless maid at last;
In humble sackcloth habit only
The nuns her blameless form had dressed.
And yet her spirit undissembling,
As when the silk brocade she wore,
By dreams unholy as before
Was agonized by shame and trembling.
Before the altar, in her cell,
Or in the hour of solemn singing,
She often heard in accents ringing
The haunting voice she knew so well.
Sometimes across the vaulted shrine,
In a mist of incense at the mass,
There suddenly a form would pass
And dimly for a moment shine.
His face shone softly as a star.
His voice allured her from afar.

3

The convent, by a hillock bounded,
Stood hidden in a lonely glen,
By stately poplar trees surrounded
And spreading sycamores; and when
The day was done and darkness fell,

The lighted taper in her cell
Shone glimmering across the glen.
And where the row of crosses rose
Above the graves in calm repose,
Daylong among the almond trees
The birds made sweetest melodies;
There leaping sportively, the fountains
And icy rills fell rippling past,
Glad in one stream to meet at last
Beneath the beetling crags of mountains
And flow together through the bowers
Covered with the rime of flowers.

4

There mountain summits loom in view.
And when at dawn the hazy blue
Curls softly in the vales of dew,
And turning to the East their faces
The muezzins cry their hour of prayer;
And when the bell their slumber chases
Resounding in the trembling air,
To wake the convent from the dream
Of night; when in the hour supreme
And pure at dawn the Gruzian maiden
Descends the mountain to the stream
With a slender water pitcher laden,—
Then far the summit of the snows
As a tender wall of lilac glows
Against the azure heavens lying.
And when at eve the sun is dying,
And veiled in rose the peaks are sighing,

Above all mountains towering far
Beyond the barriers of cloud,
Kazbék, imperial and proud,
Stands vast—a mighty crownéd tsar.

5

Tamára, by her thoughts obsessed,
Knew no response within her breast
To silent prayers of pure delight;
The world appeared a fate pursuing
Her every hour to her undoing
Alike by day and dark of night.
And oft it seemed the evening air
Rang loud with evil voices calling;
Before the holy icon falling
Tamára wept in her despair.
So wild the night with bitter weeping,
Sometimes a traveller unsleeping
Would listen, troubled, passing near,
And muse: "A spirit moans with pain,
Chained in a cavern," and in fear
Would spur his weary horse again.

6

In anguish and in trepidation,
Tamára sat oft alone before
Her window in pensive contemplation,
And gazed, as though upon a shore
Afar in azure; pale and dumb,
She heard a whisper, "He will come."
Not vainly came that dream of splendor,

Nor had her tempter come in vain
With words all magical and tender,
With eyes of yearning and of pain!
On many days her spirit suffered,
The reason to herself unknown,
For when unto the saints she offered
Her prayer, at heart to him alone
She prayed unheard. With heaving breast,
Exhausted by her strife and pain,
She nowhere found her ease, her rest,
But fear and burning grief again.
Her shoulders flushed, love in her face,
She saw the vision at her side;
Her arms ached madly to embrace,
And on her lips the kisses died.

7

When night-enshrouding mists had covered
The mountain peak and silent dale,
True to his wont, the Demon hovered
About the convent's sacred pale.
But long, oh long, he did not dare
To come into the hallowed shrine
To violate the peace divine.
A while it seemed he would forswear
His cruel purpose; long he wandered
Around the lofty walls and pondered,
While in the still and windless night
The leaves before him shook, affrighted.
But warmly glimmered in his sight
Her window by the icon lighted.

Tamára had been waiting long.
In deepest silence near and far
Came soft the strains of a guitar,
And softly too a tender song;
Like music flowing, unreturning,
Like falling tears the strains came forth,
So gently singing on this earth
As if the heavens gave them birth.
Or was it then an angel yearning
To meet, unseen, a friend of yore,
And sing to him—to ease his burning
Heart and the sufferings he bore
Alone, unspoken, in his sadness? . . .
At last the Demon knew the gladness,
The torment and the grief of love
Not felt before; in sudden fear
He strove to fly; he could not move
And slow there fell a burning tear
Upon the ground. . . . 'Tis said the same
Flagstone still lies beside the cell
Today, all calcined, where the flame
Of a burning tear upon it fell.

8

He entered, hopeful and elated,
Believing that his dreadful past
Was over, from sin emancipated,
That a new life had dawned at last.
He paused awhile in secret fear
By vague uncertainties possessed,
With pride unresting in his breast,

Before the trysting time drew near.
And lo! there stood with flaming sword
Upon the inner threshold gleaming
A guardian angel of the Lord,
His radiant brow and features beaming,
To shield the erring, trembling child
Beneath his wings. The angel smiled.
The rays of his celestial light
Fell blinding on the Demon's sight;
Instead of tender love at meeting
He heard a stern and wrathful greeting:

9

"O restless spirit of temptation,
What brings thee at this midnight hour?
Here no believer in thy power,
No slave of evil inspiration,
For they who worship at this shrine
In truth and love are wholly mine.
Who called thee forth?"
      The Demon smiled
In answer, but his brow grew black,
His flaming eyes with envy wild,
And all his ancient hate came back.
"She is mine!" He spoke with proud derision:
"She is mine! Leave her to her fate!
O guardian angel, thou art too late
And all in vain thy firm decision!
No longer here thy shrine and bride.
I now have laid my seal's impress
Upon her heart imbued with pride;

Alone I love her, alone possess!"
The angel sadly gazed, beholding
The victim with a pitying glance,
And slow, his rainbow wings unfolding,
He vanished in the sky's expanse.

10
TAMÁRA
Oh, who are you? Your words ensnare!
Who sent you? Hell or Heaven, who?
And what your will?

DEMON
          Ah, you are fair!

TAMÁRA
Who are you? I beseech you, who?

DEMON
I am the one to whom you listened,
Whose thoughts and feelings are of you,
Who whispered in the stilly night,
Whose grief you have divined, whose might
And vision in your slumber glistened.
I am one by all the living hated,
By whom all hope is desolated.
I am the scourge of men's defeat,
The bane of nature, God's enemy!
I am the lord of liberty
And thought! Behold me at your feet!
I bring to you my heart's confession,
And all my tender love and fears;
I bring my suffering and passion,

My first humility of tears.
O hear me, hear me with compassion!
By just a word you could restore
My life to heaven and to good;
Clad in your godlike love, I would
In brightness new appear before
The empyrean brotherhood.
O hear me to the last, I pray!
I love, I am your slave today!
Since first I knew you, from that hour
My immortality and power
I've hated in my heart. I confess
I envied unaware your fateful,
Imperfect earthly happiness;
To be apart from you was hateful,
To be alone was meaningless.
Then sudden in my bloodless heart
I felt the flame of ancient pangs,
And in my rankling wounds a smart
More cruel by far than serpent fangs.
What means eternity to me?
My empire, the world's immensity?
Mere sounding words, an empty dream,
A shrine without a god supreme.

   TAMÁRA
Leave me, O spirit of temptation!
Oh cease, I do not trust my foe!
Dear God above, behold my woe! ...
I cannot pray for my salvation!
Your venom rages in my heart;
It is my end at last. I die!

Your words are death to me,—depart!
You vow you love me. Tell me, why?

DEMON

Ah, fairest, why? I scarce can say.
But, ravished with new life at last,
From off my guilty brow I cast
In pride my thorny crown away.
All past is dust; my Paradise,
Or Hell, lies henceforth in your eyes.
My love for you no human passion,
No earthly feeling, but a dream
Of boundless rapture and possession
Within the mind and heart supreme.
Since God the universe created,
Since life and time began, your face
Before me lived in endless space,
In wastes of ether unabated.
Long, long ago, in days foreknown
I heard your name resounding clear,
And, when I dwelt within the sphere
Of bliss, I called but you alone.
If you could only comprehend
This nameless bitterness of living
Age after age, this unforgiving
In joy or sorrow without end,—
For evil deeds no praise receiving,
And no reward for good! For ages
To lust for self and live a life
Of emptiness, in fields of strife
That never peace nor fame assuages!
To live with hate against my will,

All knowing, nothing yet desiring,
And nothing in the world admiring,
But hating ever deeper still! . . .
When God proclaimed my great disgrace
And curse upon me, from that day
All things celestial turned away
From me and spurned my warm embrace.
Across the gulfs of ether blue
I saw the stars in festal rays
Passing upon their golden ways,
But me, their erstwhile friend, they knew
No more. I called in my distress
The outcast spirits to my side;
I heard their wrath and bitterness,
I heard their cries of hate and pride.
In terror then I fled dejected,
Not knowing where, beyond the skies;
The world was void, myself rejected
Alike by friends and Paradise.
And like a bark disabled, going
Without a rudder or a sail
Upon a stream before the gale,
I wandered, where or why not knowing.
Thus in the vaulted morning sky
A shred of thunder cloud drifts by
Dark-frowning in the azure air,
And dares not tarry anywhere,
But steals away, God only knows
From where it comes or where it goes.
Not long in might I ruled mankind,
Not long inclined their hearts to sin,

To spurn all beauty of the mind
And shame all excellence within
Their nature. No, not long. The flame
Of faith I sought to quench forever:
Were fools and knaves alone my aim
In life, my one concern forever?
How oft in mountain passes hiding
I flared up as a meteor bright
In murky darkness of the night
When lone a traveller came riding.
I heard him o'er the precipice
Fall plunging down the deep abyss,
The clouds of dust behind him trailing,
In blood and death the rocks among.
But hate and pain and human wailing
Did not avail to please me long.
How oft with wind and tempest waging
My blinding strife, in mist, or clad
In lightning and in thunder, raging
Among the clouds, I darted dread
Among the warring realms untamed,—
To quench my wounded heart's regret,
To quell my mind, and all the named
Eternal memories forget! . . .
What mean the sorrows and privations,
The labor and the cares of man
Of past and present generations,
Beside one momentary span
Of my unfathomed tribulations?
But man, poor creature born of dust,
Whose life is meaningless and brief,

May live with hope, for God is just.
He judges, yet He will forgive!
Only I with unabated grief
Until the end of time must live
Unresting with my bitter pangs.
My grief, immortal as the soul,
Now sears me as a living coal,
Now stings me as with serpent fangs,
Oppressive like a stone in gloom—
An ever imperishable tomb
Of buried passion, hope, and doom!

   TAMÁRA
Why tell your sorrows and lament
To me alone? You must atone
To God for sins—

     DEMON
       Against you? ... Repent?

   TAMÁRA
We may be heard! ...

     DEMON
       We are alone.

   TAMÁRA
But God!

     DEMON
       Is man indeed His care
On earth? Heaven, not earth, His care!

   TAMÁRA
But flames of Hell for all eternity!

DEMON
Tamára, you shall be with me!

TAMÁRA
Whoe'er you are, my friend unbidden,
Because I grieve, I listen still
To you, with true compassion hidden
Deep in my heart, against my will.
But if your aim is to deceive me,
If guile alone your secret goal,
What triumph? Oh, have pity, leave me!
What gain to you one human soul?
There are many maidens in our land
All fairer than the blooming rose,
Whose virgin couch and sweet repose
Remain untroubled by the hand
Of death. Am I more dear than those?
Nay, swear to me a sacred vow! . . .
You see how great my anguish now!
Your eyes gaze on a woman's dreams.
I would not, yet I greatly fear;
But you are knowing, wise; it seems
You needs must pity me.—O hear!
Swear on your oath, can none be spoken?
O promise me a solemn vow,—
Can sacred promises be broken?
Swear you renounce all evil now!

DEMON
I swear by the first day created,
I swear by the last day and hour,
I swear by shame and evil hated,
By truth triumphant in its power.

I swear by torments of the heart,
By dreams of exultation fleeting,
By every rapture of our meeting,
And by the hour when we must part.
I swear by all the spirit hordes
Of kindred rebel deities,
By angels of the flaming swords,
By all my watchful enemies;
I swear by Heaven and by Hell,
By all things holy in the spheres
Above, and by your last farewell;
I swear by you, by your first tears
For me, your tenderness and sighing,
And by your waving silken hair.
By happiness and pain undying,
And by my love for you, I swear
I disavow my thoughts of pride,
I disavow my vengeance blind!
I vow I shall no more misguide
By craft and wiles the human mind.
I ask to make my peace with Heaven;
I wish to love, I wish to pray
Again, I wish to be forgiven.
I would again believe in good,
And, penitential, wash away
The flames of my rebellious mood,
And let the human race at peace
In joy and labor find release.
Believe, Tamára, till this hour
No soul perceived, save I alone,
Your worth. I have chosen you my own!

I lay before your feet my power.
Your love as a boon I am awaiting;
I give you life, eternity;
I shall be as great in constancy
And love as I was great in hating.
A spirit of the trackless air,
I will enthrone you high above
The everlasting stars, my fair
First-chosen and exalted love!
Without regret and vain compassion
You shall regard this wretched earth,
Where happiness too soon grows ashen
And beauty languishes from birth,
Where crimes abound and tortures flourish,
Where passions wither year by year,
Where men no love or hatred nourish,
But live in constant craven fear.
Behold their fleeting loves, in truth
No more than pulsing blood of youth!—
Years pass away; their blood runs cold.
Whose love can strive with separation,
Resist new beauty and temptation,
Our weariness and grief of old,
Alone with dreams of adoration?
No, beloved! 'tis not your fate
To languish in a living grave
In silence, with a brutish mate,
Of cruel jealousy the slave,
Among the base and stony-hearted,
Deceiving friends and secret foes,
With empty fear and hope departed,

Vain cares and unavailing woes.
You shall not wither then in sadness
Behind stone walls, with prayer all wan,
Insensible to love and gladness,
And far alike from God and man
Removed. Tamára, you are fated
For greater bliss by destiny,
For highest love predestinated
Of suffering and ecstasy.
Forget the loveless and the dead
And leave mankind unto their fate!
I will reveal to you instead
The fountains of a purer state;
My hosts of spirits and the faery
Legions will serve you at your feet,
O lovely bride, and spirits aery
Will follow in your sovran suite.
And from the eastern star at even
I will pluck for you a golden crown,
And midnight dew and blooms of heaven
Will gleam as diamonds in your gown;
I will engird your form around
With rosy rays of sunset shining;
I will in balm and magic sound
Bestow the sunset eve enshrining
The vaster music of the air;
And I will rear a splendid chamber,
A pleasant hall with bowers rare
Of turquoises and clearest amber.
I will dive below the sea, and rise
On swiftest wings above the skies,

To give all to you of life and bliss!
Be mine, Tamára! . . .

11

With a kiss
Her trembling lips he quickly presses;
To faint entreaties he replies
With words seductive, with caresses,
Deep passion brooding in his eyes,
A searing flame. Like a sword of light
He gleamed in dark of endless night,
Relentless, poised as if to smite.
The Demon triumphed. His caress
As venom quickly pierced her heart;
An aching cry of wild distress
A moment rent the night apart,
A cry that rang a tale heart-breaking
Of suffering, and love, and strife,
Reproach, disconsolate leave-taking,—
Her sad farewell to youth and life.

12

At that late hour, a lonely sentry
Was pacing slow his wonted round
Beneath the walls when, by the entry
Of the convent cell, he heard a sound;
And slackening his pace, the kind
Old watchman paused before the gate
To listen, troubled in his mind,
His hand upon the iron plate.
In the surrounding night alone,

It seemed to him that he could hear
A sound of yielding lips, a moan,
And then a stifled cry. In fear
He waited, dreading the unknown
And deep in wonder. . . . Far and near
The night lay still; a moment sped.
Perhaps it was a fancied dream,
The whisper of a passing breeze
With murmur of the leaves in trees;
Perhaps a mournful mountain stream
Was tossing softly in its bed.
Then hurriedly he said a prayer
To quell his sinful doubts, to shun
Suspicion in his mind, the snare
Set ready by the evil one.
He crossed himself, praying for grace
Against each evil spell and sound,
And, silent, strode with quicker pace
Again upon his wonted round. . . .

13

In beauty like a peri dreaming,
Tamára in her coffin lay,
And whiter than her cover gleaming
Her pallid brow, as clear as day.
Forever closed her eyes in sleep. . . .
But who, O Heaven, would not say
A lover's kiss or dawn of day
Would not awaken her from dreaming,
Her death an unsubstantial seeming?
But all in vain the golden rays

Caress her, and for many days
In vain, with speechless grief and sighs,
Her kinsfolk kiss those lips and eyes.
No power, not of human breath
Or hand, can break the seal of death!

14

Never before Tamára's dresses
Had shown so rich and rainbow-bright,
Not even on her festal night!
Wild native flowers in her tresses,
As ancient usages demand,
And blooms held tightly in her hand
Sent lovingly their sweetness forth,
As if they bade farewell to earth!
So still she lay, her pallid face
Bore no intimation nor a trace
Of her last ecstasy and passion;
The peace of beauty and of grace
Appeared imprisoned in her face
Serene with marbled cold dispassion,
Devoid of feeling, mind, or breath,
Mysterious as the face of death.
A smile surpassing strange, congealing,
Lay fleeting as a shadow lies,
Too visibly great grief revealing
To all discerning, watchful eyes;
There fleeted on her lips, disdainful,
A spirit long resigned to die,
The mind's expression of a painful
Experience, and a mute goodbye.

That smile declared her earthly being
Was but a lifeless form, unseeing,
Deserted, never to arise,
The light extinguished in her eyes.
Thus, when the sun is sinking low
In glowing waves of molten gold,
The mountain peaks still briefly hold
The glimmer of the afterglow;
But icy heights in dying light
Send forth no comfort in their rays,
No hope into the desert night
For men who walk the barren ways.

15

A crowd of kin and friends assembled
To take Tamára to her rest.
In his despair, with hands that trembled,
And beating wild his aged breast,
Her father mounted then his horse.
The long procession, sad and slow,
In silence moved upon its course
Three days, three nights, in wind and snow.
Among the tombs of kinsfolk brave,
They had prepared Tamára's grave.
Goudal's forefather of long ago,
Who raided many a helpless village,
Had vowed, when illness struck him low,
In penance for his deeds of pillage,
To build a chapel on a lonely
Mountain peak of snow, where only
The vultures of the desert soar,

Where storm winds shrilly sing and roar.
And soon amid the towering snows
A solitary shrine had risen—
A robber's body to emprison
And give his bones their last repose.
The mountain crag of cloud and sound
Became a human burial ground,
As though the grave is warmer, dearer
Afar from bustling crowds, and nearer
To God—with peace eternal crowned.
Vain thought! The dead will not again
Dream days of happiness or pain. . . .

16

In azure skies of boundless space
The guardian angel, glorifying
God, upon golden wings was flying,
And within his merciful embrace
He bore a sinful soul. Her fears
With tender words of consolation
He washed away with angel tears
And song of heavenly salvation.
They heard celestial strains resounding
From realms of Paradise afar,
When, sudden, in the air surrounding
The Demon soared, their way to bar.
His might was like a whirlwind loud;
He shone as lightning flashes shine,
And in his frenzied rage, with loud
Defiance, thundered, "She is mine!"

She clasped the Angel in her fear
And terror of the Demon close
Who challenged in the starry sphere
Her fate for bliss or woe. He rose
Before her, dreadful and morose
In ancient might. His glance of flame
Was full of vengeance and of wrath,
With hatred vast upon his breath;
A charnel house of hate, his frame
Was unchangeable and bleak as death.

"Hence, fiend of darkness!" in reply
Rang out afar the Angel's voice:
"No more shall powers of Hell rejoice!
The hour of judgment now is nigh,
And God is merciful on high.
Her days of suffering are fled;
Fallen the chains of sin she hated,
And all her wrongs and faults are dead.
Her coming we have long awaited.
So brief her life, her life of sorrow
And dull immovable despair,
Her spirit mounting from her birth
To God in dreams of bliss each morrow!
God made her soul surpassing fair,
And wove her chords in light and love;
Not fated for the loveless earth
Her radiant and gentle air.
She has redeemed with bitter sighs
And tears her doubts—to rise above

Her suffering, and Paradise
Receives today its child of love!"
The Angel on the Tempter bending
With stern reproval in his eyes,
Spread wide his wings, in joy ascending
Across the ether of the skies.
The Demon cursed his loss and yearning,
The mad, wild dream his fancy wove;
Alone, with pride of spirit burning,
Alone in space, all living spurning,
He stood,—devoid of hope or love! . . .

✸ ✸ ✸

Upon a steep and craggy hill
Above the valley of Koishour,
Today a wayfarer can still
Behold in ruins an ancient tower,
And hear the legends that amaze
The young; by rumor and tradition
It stands a speechless apparition,
A witness of enchanted days,
Grim-frowning in the trees. Darkling
It looms, while in the vale below
The village huts and fields lie sparkling
With meadows green where blossoms glow,
With mingled hum of men, and rumbling
Of caravans upon their way,
With rushing streams and rapids tumbling
In sparkling foam and silver spray.
With smiles and gladdening young voices

There life eternally rejoices,
All careless, like a child in fun,
With coolness, dew, and springtime sun.

All dark the castle stands, its glory
Still lingering beyond its prime,
Like an aged man alone and hoary
Surviving all his friends in time.
Alone its habitants await
The rising moon with evening light,
To swarm abroad and celebrate
With buzzing glee the phantom night:
The spider like a hermit grey
Begins his web of warp and woof;
A group of lizards darting play
Unheeding on the sunken roof;
From a gloomy crevice of his hiding
Along the broken porch of stone
The wary snake comes slowly gliding,
Now curled in triple rings, now grown
Into a gleaming stripe, abiding
Like a brightly shining sword found
Abandoned upon a battle ground
In grass. . . . There's nothing to remind
One of the past left long behind,
Effaced with care by time where all
Remains now desolate and wild.
No longer lives in fame Goudál,
Or fair Tamára, his lovely child.

But still the chapel to this hour

Stands high upon the mountain peak
Among the clouds and boulders bleak,
Protected by some holy power.
Beside its gate, in silent might,
Stand as on watch dark granite shapes
Hidden beneath their snowy capes,
And on their breasts, like armor bright,
Eternal ice in blazing light.
The massive boulders without number
Hang vast and frowning like a wall,
As if the frost had chained in slumber
The avalanches in their fall.
And there the blizzard on its round
Whirls high the snow as dust in flying,
Then chants a weary droning sound
Unto the ice-bound sentries crying.
The news about that church divine
Goes round the earth, and lone the clouds
From out the East in pilgrim crowds
Come trooping to the wondrous shrine;
But no one comes a tear to shed,
To mourn Goudál, or Tamára dead.
Kazbék in giant gloom guards ever
His prize within his icy breast,
And man's unresting life will never
Disturb their everlasting rest.

1841